BRAIN STORM

AN ELECTRIFYING JOURNEY

KATE RECORE

Robert D. Reed Publishers

Robert D. Reed Publishers . Bandon, OR

Robert D. Reed Publishers
P.O. Box 1992
Bandon, OR 97411
Phone: 541-347-9882; Fax: -9883
E-mail: 4bobreed@msn.com
Website: www.rdrpublishers.com

Editors: Stuart Horowitz, Nancy Wilson, and Cleone Reed
Cover: Andy Taylor, theparkcreative.com
Formatter: Cleone Reed

Soft Cover: 978-1-944297-46-6
EBook: 978-1-944297-47-3

Library of Congress Control Number: 2019902817

Designed and Formatted in the United States of America

DEDICATION

To Mom and Dad,
for saving my life,
and to Brian and Jake,
for giving it meaning.

ACKNOWLEDGMENTS

Family first. My family loves me, and I love them, without exception or question. They have weathered all the storms I've been through, and have steadied my boat along the way. My parents and siblings pushed me forward up the hill without allowing me to turn back. They kept me here.

Next, Dr. David Labiner. Without the care of my current neurologist, I probably wouldn't be alive. He is a true hero in my life's story.

Also my friends. I have been blessed with many people who reached out and pulled me up when I struggled to keep my head above water. My life is rich with friends who laugh with me and at me, and love me anyway. I thank them for the steady support they've given me throughout life and this writing process. In particular, Erin, who convinced me I had a story worth sharing. I never would've written this book without her belief in me.

Thank you also to Stuart Horowitz and Nancy Wilson, my amazing editors. You should've seen this before. And thanks to Andy Taylor for the stunning book cover. It is a gift to have such talented siblings. Thanks also to Cleone Reed for reminding me to breathe when I need to throughout the publishing process.

Finally, my reasons for everything, Brian and Jake. The purpose they've given to my life defies description. They give me unconditional encouragement to write, and are my kindest editors. I would be pointless, irrelevant without them. They make my life shiny.

Contents

INTRODUCTION

Imagine sitting alone in a stranger's house. No voices chatter in another room. No promising smells drift from the kitchen. You sit in solitude, taking in the artifacts of another person's life. An interesting lamp sits on the table. You wonder where it came from. A red plastic clock on the wall ticks away the seconds, while a little cat perched on the bookshelf steals your attention. It looks old and tattered, some whiskers missing on one side. There must be a story there.

Now imagine the stranger's house is actually yours. According to the lease, you've lived there for a year, alone. But you don't know where the lamp next to you came from. Did you buy it last week, or did your grandfather leave it to you when he died? Why would you own such a relentless clock? The story behind the little cat, however tender it may be, has been forever lost, a victim of your inadequate brain.

A constant flow of fleeting questions haunted me when I lost my memory. I lived my life like the second night in a hotel. Scraps of familiarity clung to many of my things, but their details eluded me. I recognized my table, my chairs, my bed, but I couldn't place anything into context, or remember where anything came from. Personal things, books and pictures, could have belonged to anyone but me. My past was vacant.

Even today, I can't remember the places I've been. Sitting at the family Christmas table a few years ago, I learned I had been to Bermuda. I would not have guessed I'd seen those pink beaches if someone else hadn't pulled a story from their memory at that table. I've lost most of my family history.

I keep a shelf of Shakespeare I remember nothing about. When I re-read something, my mind is too permanently riddled with holes to retain the story for more than a few months. I keep a list of movies I've seen, books I've read, television shows I like. I give them ratings, so when someone asks me if I've "read that," or "seen this," I can answer, and even tell them if I liked the pictures or the words.

There are a few things so rooted in my reality they cannot be yanked out. Those things become very clear, detailed and isolated like ice cubes in a punch bowl on a hot day or black seeds in a bright red slice of watermelon. Most of the moments I remember circle around trauma, scary things, and low points. I have only a few happy childhood memories.

I do clearly remember, even now, my clothes. I see photos of myself as a child and have no idea where they were taken, or who the other people are. But I remember the stiffness of the fabric my pants were made from, or the way the buttons on the shirt were a little too large for their buttonholes, or how hot my feet felt in the shoes. I will think to myself, *That boy must have been my prom date. I don't remember his name. I do remember how much I loved that dress. We couldn't believe it when we found those shoes that perfectly matched the soft pink color.*

Such a "girl" thing, I might think for a fleeting second, before sternly scolding my mind's need to categorize into gender-specific norms. I remind myself, *you don't have to be a girl to love clothes.* I know first-hand how dangerous labels can be.

Since the age of twenty-three, I have spent my life fighting against being categorized as a "girl." My life literally depended upon proving I needed to be treated as a genderless patient, rather than an over-dramatic, hysterical young woman. My tests were ambiguous at best, not worthy of the conclusions drawn about me. And I was far from alone.

Dangerous misconceptions about women very often delay or entirely prevent us from receiving necessary medical attention. Even today, doctors again and again base diagnoses on the perception that girls think there is something wrong with them physically, when hormones and a need for attention are to blame.

I have yet to meet another woman who has not experienced some level of gender bias in an examining room. We accept this as the way things work.

Before my misdiagnosis, I never considered whether or not I felt I received different medical treatment or advice than a man. I never thought to examine the implications of being considered the weaker sex by the medical community. I wish I had considered the appropriateness of that norm before I ever had a seizure. I may have started my journey with a different doctor, in a different direction.

If my condition had been treated earlier, I may not have lost my memory of every book I read or movie I saw before the age of twenty-four. If the doctors from whom I sought care had helped me instead of dismissing me, I may never have known the loneliness and fear that came from being a stranger in my own story.

Instead of caring for me, doctors tried to shame me into believing I chose to lose any connection with my life. They insisted I self-induced my seizures, or "imagined"—lied—about them, to get attention from my parents. I had not lived with my parents since I was seventeen, and I had lived in two other states. Still, doctors insisted I thrived on my mother's and father's attentions.

Tired, sick, injured, and scared, I had to fight to prove I was worth helping. Like many young women with unusual symptoms, I pounded on doors shut in my face by neurologists who decided I only needed mental health care the minute they saw "anxiety disorder" in my records. I had to wage war against a specialty dominated by men.

Not all wars are clearly defined. They are not all chess boards neatly covered with black and white squares and players respectfully taking turns. True battlefields are gray and mottled. Right and wrong don't stand politely and wait their turns. They wear disguises. In the battle for my life, they called themselves doctors.

Of course my memory from those years holds many imperfections. But the sharp moments of my shattered past remain painfully clear. To write this book, I relied on my journals, my friends and family, and my medical records to place these shards back together into a story I can share.

ACT I:

A GATHERING STORM

Only when I fall do I get up again.

~ Vincent Van Gogh, painter and epileptic

Chapter 1—Running In Bed

Jolting awake, I sat straight up in the darkness, filled with desperation. I heard a sound in my room—someone moving. I was not alone. I sat frozen, taking sips of air as quietly as I could. Who was it? And where was I?

I widened my eyes and searched the darkness for something familiar. Staring around the room I distinguished each shadowy shape and put it into place in my mind. There was my dresser strewn with inexpensive jewelry, my clothes on the floor where I dropped them before climbing into bed, my bedside table stacked with books. I studied the layout of the room, where the door and window were. I remembered I was in my new apartment, where I was living alone for the first time. But I wasn't alone at that moment.

I checked in with myself to be sure I wasn't dreaming. *"I am Katie Scarlett Taylor, twenty-three, Tucson, Arizona, in my new apartment."* I was definitely sitting up and fully awake.

I considered calling out to my uninvited visitor but could not think of anything to say. As my ears dialed in, I determined that the sound came from somewhere very close to me. I realized the sound came from my bed.

I threw back my covers. My leg was moving, jumping erratically, without any conscious signal from my brain. Shocked and helpless, I watched my leg running in my bed without me. Blood began pounding in my ears as I began to panic. My lungs and heart raced, seeming too large for my chest.

The movement stopped as suddenly as it started. My leg woke up and resumed a normal relationship with my conscious brain. I wiggled my toes and bent my knee up and down. Ordinary responses. My breathing and heartbeat slowed. I felt like I had sprinted a mile.

Next, a pile of uninvited emotions tumbled on top of me. I felt guilt for not listening to my mother, who didn't want me to live alone. Loneliness came next, single and on no real career path. Sadness at losing my friends to the end of college, watching them move on one by one. Self-deprecation because only losers like me stayed in the same place they had lived all their lives. And finally, panic about being alone in more ways than one.

My thoughts slowed and heavy depression instantly followed, settling in my chest like spent tears. Who was I?

When my alarm went off, I didn't know I'd been sleeping. I thought I was still awake and staring at my clock, counting the minutes until I needed to get out of bed and get on with my day.

The morning brought inevitable desert sunshine and rational thought. The night before seemed silly, the emotions dream-like. I felt absolutely fine, back to my glass-half-full self. I could not imagine why I had suddenly been so unhappy when things were going so well. I finally had my very own apartment without roommates to deal with, and working for my father was not as bad as I thought it might be. My only worries in life centered around choosing between good options and picking which dreams to follow.

My writing had traveled in an exciting direction. My father's former talent agent who represented him when he was a young stand-up comedian now had an impressive position at one of the most well-respected talent agencies in L.A. He sent my screenplays to their readers, and they had recommended two for consideration. He offered to represent me but told me I had to relocate to L.A. I had half-heartedly considered the opportunity, balancing the slim possibility of being taken seriously in the movie business with my love for acting on the stage. I was told that in the movie business, writers were writers (and were usually men,) and actors were actors. The order of things held significant importance in show business. Acting needed to come first. I put off making the move to L.A., convincing myself writing would wait until I established myself as an actress.

As an actress, my dreams revolved around the other coast. I couldn't see myself on a movie screen, but I could visualize standing on a Broadway stage, looking out across the heads of unrecognizable theater-goers, their faces hidden by the stage lights shining in my eyes. Even though I had friends living there from when I performed summer Shakespeare in Vermont, New York was very far away, even more unforgiving than Hollywood, and expensive. I knew I would have a better chance at getting roles there if I improved my résumé first.

Actors relied heavily on each other to find jobs in new markets. A good word from a respected fellow actor meant a foot in the door. A theater in Denver—where I also had connections from another actor I had worked with—seemed like a safer first step in the direction I intended to go. That's where I had set my sights. I just needed to figure out how to get there by summer, so I could move with my friend Kim. She was the last of my friends from college, and she thought Denver sounded like a great change of scenery.

With everything falling easily into place, why did I feel so much doubt in myself the night before? How could a moving leg make me feel such a void?

Searching for unsnagged pantyhose, I reminded myself the simplest reasons usually fit best: It had been a bad dream. It certainly was not the first time sleep woke me up.

I excelled at nightmares. In my dreams people died horrible deaths. Blood and gore abounded, and I often got hurt or even killed. Nothing about my dreams made sense. Mythical animals attacked me, and I had to keep children quiet while I hid them from the Grim Reaper wearing full Native-American dress and riding a bloody horse. I found dead animals I forgot to care for and could never get anywhere on time. Dreams never brought beauty and hope and happiness to the landscape of my mind. By daylight, a running leg seemed benign in comparison. I decided my leg had obviously acted out a new kind of nightmare that involved my body.

I showered, dressed, and stepped outside. Deceptively cool mornings make February feel almost wintery in the Sonoran Desert. I hugged my sweater around my shoulders, knowing I would discard any extra clothing in an hour. Air conditioners woke up earlier than normal that year, with winter days in the nineties.

I instinctively avoided holding the metal railing as I descended the concrete stairs. I was a desert girl, familiar with the rules that come with living where temperatures frequently top one-hundred degrees. In a few months, the metal would be hot enough to blister hands.

Without freeways or highways, and with flocks of retired "snowbirds" landing in the winter months who are not in a hurry to get anywhere, Tucson required patience behind the wheel. At least they usually avoided the roads during morning rush hour. Traffic signals and surface streets stretched the entire way to Taylor Advertising, which filled the tenth floor of the tallest of the two buildings downtown. I always dreaded the slow, boring commute ahead of me.

I did not realize then what a privilege driving would become.

Chapter 2—Replay

I checked in with myself to be sure I was not dreaming. *"I am Katie Scarlett Taylor, twenty-three, Tucson, Arizona, in my new apartment."* I was definitely sitting up and fully awake.

My leg was moving, but I was not moving it. Sudden stillness. Emotions smothered me. Everything was soaked in déjà vu, the dismal feelings seeming familiar but distant. I fell back into a restless sleep.

I did not remember until the morning that I'd had the same experience a few days before. The entire "dream" felt brand new while it was happening. Even the sight of my leg moving had stirred no actual memory—just a sense of familiarity.

Again, daylight brought the sensation of past dreams. Another hot day in February had begun. What would the summer bring if today topped out at ninety-one, as predicted? With that much heat that early in the year July could be apocalyptic. I would be in Denver by then, of course, away from the misery of desert heat.

I planned to meet friends after work. Just a few hours at the office answering phones until my real life began, with bourbon-and-sevens, and dancing until the music stopped and the lights came on. Then, my friends and I would finish off the evening by going to Village Inn for huge piles of greasy food before finally heading home.

Life was good. I had friends at work who liked to go to happy hour and didn't treat me like the boss's daughter. I laughed and lived life, forgetting about my interrupted sleep until I crawled into bed at night.

My running-leg incidents came and went sporadically and always seemed trivial by daylight. I could not think of any way or any reason to tell anyone. No one would care, except my mother. She would probably ask me about it for days, and try to convince me I should not be alone because no one would know if I needed help in the middle of the night. She would think my leg's movements resulted from some serious condition. She often planted seeds of uncertainty and insecurity in my mind that took root and grew. I was the full part of the glass, and she was the empty. I did not need her to make me even more concerned about myself.

My mother did not like for me to live with a roommate, much less without one. She couldn't imagine why I would enjoy living alone. She begged me to call her when I got home at night, as I had in college. I refused, even though I sometimes felt fearful crossing the parking lot and entering my little apartment late at night. I usually left more lights burning than necessary and checked the windows for shadows before ascending the stairs.

I needed to think of myself as independent enough to live in my own space. I did my best to convince myself I could handle anything that came my way. After several weeks, when the movements spread into my other leg and the disruptive emotions began to linger into my mornings, my confidence eroded.

I thought about making a doctor's appointment but wasn't sure what he would possibly tell me. What would anyone tell me? I ignored the problem, and hoped it would all go away as suddenly as it started.

Chapter 3—Moving Parts

My arms started moving next. The entire right side of my body jerked. Afterward, my right arm and leg would feel numb, like they were "asleep" from lack of blood flow. They were coming several times a week, sometimes several times a night. I knew then it was my brain. Something felt very wrong inside my head.

The inevitable emotions became more burdensome than the physical experience. Depression began to seep into my days, amplified by the monotony of my job saying "Good morning/afternoon, Taylor Advertising" over and over. The people I worked with managed to turn my mood around by midday; but forcing myself out of bed after an emotional, sleepless night, getting dressed and driving to the office could be painful.

I began to feel anxious when I got into bed, wondering if I would sleep through the night. I felt exhausted all day, and started losing patience with everything and everyone. Sleep deprivation slowed my mental function. Emotions, memory, and cognition all felt the effects of my limited sleep.

As a child and young adult, I never required much sleep. I could function well with four or five hours per night. But sleeping short hours combined with repeatedly waking up and not being able to go back to sleep was becoming a health crisis. I tried to fit enough hours together before and after being charged awake to make a night's sleep. Now, days were growing longer as spring approached, and my windows began to glow earlier. If I was awake when the sun came up, I rarely fell back to sleep. And my days didn't allow for naps.

The clock became my enemy. If I woke up between four and five, I would watch the digital numbers change until the alarm went off at seven. Something about my sleep rhythm prevented me from slipping back into slumber between those hours.

I needed to get back to my normal sleep pattern. I decided to see my doctor.

#

Describing my symptoms to the nurse at my general practitioner's office proved to be difficult. I sounded ridiculous, even to myself. My legs were moving at night, waking me from sleep. And now sometimes my arm moved, too. If ever there was a "Lay off the drugs, take two aspirin and sleep it off" moment in her career, this had to be it. I could visualize her eye-roll over the phone.

Regardless, I insisted on scheduling a visit. The nurse begrudgingly scheduled me with the nurse practitioner. Even that appointment required I wait for a week. I began to play a frustrating game with healthcare that would continue for years.

#

To get the most from the insurance system, my doctor's practice maintained thousands of active patients. Seeing my doctor always meant first having an appointment to see his nurse practitioner, then scheduling a time to return for a second appointment with him. That day, I knew I would not be seeing a doctor.

After a robust wait in the lobby, reading magazines I never had time for in the real world, the nurse practitioner stepped out of the examining area, called my name, and then led me to a bright, predictably furnished examining room. I perched on the end of the examination table, describing my symptoms while she took my blood pressure.

I didn't know how to tell her what was happening to me. A moving leg or two and swinging arm at night seemed almost comical. The sensations surrounding the experiences, so powerful to me, were difficult to describe, and words were hard to put together.

I always found the nurse practitioner to be a competent, reliable provider of basic care. She could get prescriptions signed and pass out antibiotics with the best of them. When I described my symptoms to her this time, she looked puzzled, and asked me to wait. Then she came back and told me the doctor would be in.

Actual visits with the doctor were reserved for serious illnesses that went beyond sore throats and skin rashes. What could this be? Obviously, the NP thought it worth putting me into the inner circle. I waited several minutes longer.

I really liked my doctor. He had known me since I was fifteen. He treated my entire family. I trusted him, literally, with my life.

I cheerfully accepted the peck on the cheek and told him, as quickly as I could, about my rogue limbs. I knew I did not actually have an appointment with him and did not want to waste his time.

He listened to me carefully, asked a couple of quick questions, then smiled and patted my knee. He quickly assured me it was simply stress. As long as it happened only during sleep, and I did not have severe, debilitating headaches, there was no need for concern. I just needed to find a way to lower the stress in my life.

He wished me well and asked me to give his best to my parents, but I told him I did not want them to know about my sleep issues because they would be worried about me. He agreed that sounded like a good choice.

My doctor gave me a clean bill of health, and I had no reason to doubt him. A weight was lifted off my shoulders, and I could go on without a worry in the world.

I waited several days for an appointment, spent over an hour in his office, less than five minutes in his presence. In that miniscule amount of his time I felt guilty for keeping him from his other patients. I looked at them as I walked out, knowing I only had stress, and wanting to apologize for making their wait longer.

I realized the diagnosis was obvious. I knew stress did all kinds of things to our bodies, but this kind of sleep disturbance was not something I had heard of before. My feeling that the impulses were coming from my head was correct, but the cause was psychological, not physical. I just had to find a way to control my feelings and I would be back to normal.

I had absolute trust in doctors at that point. I did not question his assessment. He told me exactly what I wanted to hear. I was so relieved. Not a brain tumor! I was not going to die! I just had to find a way to be less stressed. Simple. I took in a breath full of April as I left.

Spring in the desert brings color in surprising places. Olive drab and tan are accessorized with brilliant yellows, oranges, and reds. Impossible pinks began to warm the sky in the evenings. Mornings no longer required sweaters. The world sang.

#

My brother Andy was the first person to actually see me have one of my strange dreams. We both worked at my father's ad agency and were in Colorado Springs with my parents on a family vacation disguised as a business trip.

Andy and I fit into the middle of the kids in our family. My older sister, Nancy, was newly married and starting a family of her own. My youngest brother, Dan, was finishing his junior year of high school. I was far apart enough in age, my sister four years older and my brothers four and seven years younger, to never attend the same school with any of them. We spun in our own orbits, not crossing paths often. Working with Andy at the office allowed us to get to know each other a bit, and we had become closer. But I had never discussed my strange dreams with him, or my sister or other brother. They were in the dark along with my parents.

That weekend in Colorado my brother and I shared a hotel room, and the first night we were there, I woke him up by tossing

24

and turning in the bed next to his. He thought I was having a bad dream, until I started making a low, strange noise. My body became stiff and then started jerking. It didn't last long enough for him to react, to call anyone or yell for help. I went back to sleep immediately, and so did he, assuming I had some weird kind of dream.

He teased me during breakfast with my parents the next morning. "You looked like a dying rabbit." The description he gave all of us followed along with what I thought I experienced. I felt my legs and arms jerking for a few minutes, then fell back to sleep. I didn't know about the noise I made. That was a weird, unexpected facet.

"Nice. Thanks." It was a bit embarrassing, but my dad and I laughed. My mom did not.

Because Andy had no way of knowing the way I was struggling with sleep, he hadn't thought to pay much attention to what happened the night before. Regardless, my always overly-concerned mom interrogated my brother about what he saw until my dad couldn't take any more.

"Okay, enough. He told you what he saw. Let's get going."

"Yes, let's. Please," I begged.

Everything possible to say about thirty seconds that happened in the middle of the night had been said more than once. And Colorado beckoned.

Chapter 4—Stress

I began waking with long scratches on my arms and torso. I wore mittens to bed. I cut my long nails short. I made excuses at first, saying I had accidentally scratched myself here and there. Inside I chastised myself. What was wrong with me? Why would I do this to myself? Why was I so stressed?

I expected simply knowing I could control what was happening through mental effort, just calming down and not being uptight, would instantly help me sleep normally. An enormous amount of pressure was placed on me with that diagnosis. As I continued to struggle, I was convinced it was entirely my fault. Even though I was exercising more, studying biofeedback, and improving my diet, I was apparently still too stressed. I was not doing what I had to do to make it all stop. What was that, exactly?

I decided to go for hikes to reacquaint myself with the natural world. The beauty of the majestic saguaro and the grainy sands of the arroyos, still dry and cool from the winter, did soothe my soul. But the feeling never lasted. My peace disintegrated into exhaustion by the time I reached home. When late spring arrived and the mornings began to feel like afternoons, I drifted toward the shady places, along with everyone else. Hiking lost its appeal.

I could not hide my scratches in Tucson in April. Long sleeves became suspicious when even morning temperatures rose above 80 degrees. I had to confess bits and pieces to everyone around me. Because sleep is a mysterious state for most people, filled with unexpected thoughts and strange, unaccountable hours, everyone seemed willing to accept my explanation for my scratches as "something weird happening when I dream."

#

I woke to a pillow stained with blood. Was it really blood? What else could it be? Where did it come from? I'd bitten my tongue badly, but a bite on your tongue couldn't soak a third of your pillow, could it?

It had obviously come from my mouth, diluted by saliva, spreading from dark to light. Only one terrifying answer came to my mind. I was dying.

Whether physically or psychologically, I knew at this point that the root of my misery grew in my brain. But how did blood come from my brain to my mouth? Did I forget something important about anatomy? Thinking too hard, trying to access any knowledge left me numb.

My head hurt—a thick, muddy pain instead of the sharp migraines I had dealt with for years, or the hangovers I occasionally brought upon myself. Fighting this new heaviness in my head seemed pointless. It was so hard to concentrate.

My greatest fear was dying suddenly from an aneurysm. When I was young, a child of our preacher at church, a young girl a few years older than me, suddenly disappeared from this world after having an aneurysm. The thought of being lost in an instant to an explosion in my brain, no goodbyes, terrified me. Could this be more serious than stress? Could the doctor be mistaken?

I became more emotional with my family and friends. I fantasized that every time I saw them could be the last. I knew my thoughts were over-dramatic, but sleeplessness and rational thought were not friends.

I made another appointment to see my physician. No, I told the scheduler, I did not want to see the nurse practitioner. I had already seen her. I wanted to schedule a rare actual appointment with my actual doctor. They would have to figure it out with the HMO; that wasn't my job.

Health Maintenance Organizations enjoyed great popularity in the 1990's. Originally, the concept seemed sound. Lowering the occurrence of unnecessary doctor visits and refining the choice of tests a patient goes through in turn lowers the cost of healthcare for all. However, the way the HMO's worked with doctors corrupted the system. The most profit for doctors and hospitals came from the least amount of care they offered. My doctors received yearly bonuses based on the number of referrals they provided and the expensive tests they recommended. Not for the most referrals and tests but for the least. The less care they offered, the more money they made. They received a stipend for every HMO customer they had enrolled as their patient, regardless of whether they actually offered care for that patient. With HMO's, medicine became an even more lucrative money-making career choice. But patient care suffered, and misdiagnoses rose as satisfaction dropped. My doctor lost money every time he recommended a test for me or sent me to a specialist. Thanks to my HMO, the choice between being a healer and being an entrepreneur undermined the quality of my doctors.

#

While I waited for the date, I cried lonely tears at night. Had I feared that horrific end of having an explosion in my brain since childhood because I had predicted my future? I worried my stress would speed the process, so I chastised myself for crying. I never imagined discussing my fears about my fate with anyone, because I knew my conviction seemed nonsensical. People do not predict their deaths. A headache and bites on my tongue did not foretell a sudden death. I had seen my doctor, and he told me I only had stress. Anything more serious wouldn't just happen while I slept. I would experience the same things randomly throughout the day. Why go back? I knew it did not make sense. But rationality became a luxury I couldn't afford at that point in my life.

I managed to appear to function normally during the day. Keeping my uncertainty to myself allowed me to shove worries into corners of my waking mind. I tried to go about my life without exposing too much of my uncertainty over my health.

As my doctor's appointment approached, I rehearsed what I would say in the few minutes I would be allotted to see him. I needed to tell him something different than I had the first time, so I could justify being there again. I knew I would have only a few minutes to tell him everything I needed him to know.

#

My new symptoms did not impress my doctor. He still believed I suffered from stress. But he did decide to give me a referral to see a neurologist, just in case. By giving me a referral to see a specialist, he would lose money, but by passing me along to his friend who would benefit, he could also possibly benefit in the long run by receiving referrals in return. My referral entered the machine.

A couple of years prior to my uncontrollable moving parts, I began suffering from the most common type of neurological condition: Migraines. Mine were sharp and sudden, a brain freeze, like what you experience when you eat ice cream too quickly. My headaches came without the ice cream. Without warning, I felt as though an icepick had been stabbed into my head. They were short and sudden, and terrifying. I thought then that something serious was wrong with my brain. The neurologist I saw diagnosed me with episodic vascular migraines. Having a name for them made them more tolerable. But the experience made me hesitant to make a big deal out of my running leg. I felt no pain, other than dull throbbing headaches and bites on my tongue, so I might be having another unusual type of migraine. Could it be just stress after all? But my doctor had agreed to the referral, which was rare. He must, I decided, think I should go.

Before my appointment with a neurologist came around, the convulsions increased and took over my whole body. I crawled out of bed in the morning, more exhausted than I had been while climbing in the night before. Sleep deprivation started to become my normal mode of operation. For the first time in my life, I fantasized all day about taking naps.

Four months after my battle began, I finally saw a neurologist.

Chapter 5—From Stress to Anxiety

If I could take back my first conversation with my first neurologist, I believe my life would be different today. He was the same man I had seen before for my icepick migraines. He did not really seem to remember me, although he pretended to. I had only met him once, so I did not expect him to know me.

"So, you've been having convulsions in your legs at night. Now, you are aware of these episodes, or someone else told you about them?"

Neurologists love the word episode. It sounds like a soda pop when they say it, bubbly and refreshing.

"Have you been under stress?" Well, I wasn't exactly feeling bubbly or refreshed by my "episodes."

By the time I visited him, I was experiencing several events every week. Fear, frustration, and exhaustion made me an emotional mess. Yes, I certainly felt stressed.

I remember bits and pieces of my meeting with him. With inadequate sleep, my memory continued to absorb less and less. I struggled to sound intelligent—something that had not been difficult for me in the past. Conversing with him, or with anyone, required enormous concentration.

He sat on a rolling stool while I perched on an examination table. He asked me to perform a few simple tasks—touch my nose with each finger, follow his finger with my eyes, up, down, side to side, while he held a clipboard and pen.

He was handsome, even dashing, with thick salt-and-pepper hair, and he spoke with a Spanish accent. I felt awkward talking to an older man about what happened while I slept at night. He remained very professional and austere, unaware of my hesitation. I tried to be as clear and clinical as possible while describing my most vulnerable and intimate hours, and tried to accurately relay how brutally my nights destroyed my days. I remember becoming emotional and crying a few tears at some point.

He interviewed me quite thoroughly. Some of his questions stung a bit but seemed fair. What was I doing with my life? Did I have any plan at all?

I had big plans but lived a simple life at that point. I knew what I wanted to be, what I wanted to do, where I wanted to be, but I lived day-to-day, going to work, still hanging out with friends as often as possible.

He listened without rushing me. I dug deeper and told him I still did occasional work for the theater I helped establish in town, and acted in some local radio and television ads. I focused my extra time on screenwriting, at that point. I mentioned I had been offered an opportunity as a screenwriter in L.A., but that I felt I needed to get back to the stage full-time, and to turn my focus away from writing and back to acting.

But what was my plan? He pressed me to commit to a course of action. I was twenty-three, right? Out of school? What did I actually want to be when I grew up, and wasn't it time for me to do that?

Apparently, acting and writing were not what he considered real jobs. He was not the first person in my life to think that artistic pursuits were for students and housewives and retirees. I knew the conversation well, and I took it in stride.

I opened up a bit more and told him about how I had put my life on hold. I wanted to move to Denver with my friend, Kim. She was already planning to go, so it was a perfect opportunity for me to live there because I'd have a roommate from the beginning. She was one of my favorite people, and I looked forward to living with her.

I elaborated to make the move sound like furthering my education, telling him I also had a friend I met while working with a professional theatre company who had connections to a

31

Denver theater school. He had offered to help me get a job or a spot in the graduate program when I was ready. I always loved the mountains, and Denver seemed a perfect fit for me. But my mysterious health crisis and over-protective parents kept me mired in Tucson.

He pressed me on my claims against my parents, asking me frank questions. I was out of college and twenty-three, yet I felt it was my parents' fault I still lived in Tucson without a real job? I explained that they would not help support me if I moved, and I would have to find a way to make enough money to pay for a move and possibly school. Being a receptionist did not bring in a big paycheck. I could not even think about moving until I figured out what was happening to me physically.

Those words changed my fate. In his eyes, by blaming my parents for what he saw as my inadequacies, I'd diagnosed myself.

He sent me for an EEG. He told me it would tell us if there was something actually physically happening in my brain. He would contact me with the results.

An electroencephalogram, (EEG) measures the electrical activity in the brain. A technician conducts the test, and a doctor reads the results. The brain waves are measured using small metal electrodes attached to the scalp using ultrasonic gel, or using a cap with electrodes attached inside. The test takes twenty to thirty minutes, and is completely painless. First used in the 1920's, the EEG remains the premier test for detecting epileptic brain transmissions. Unfortunately, this is not an exceptionally accurate test. If you have the type of epilepsy that responds to stimuli like flashing lights or loud noises, the technician can induce seizure activity and measure your brain abnormalities. However, if you have a brain that operates normally when you are not having a seizure, the EEG will not record anything remarkable, unless you have a seizure during the test. However, EEGs still enjoy popularity because they are compact and portable, and the results are instant, unlike an MRI or CT.

When the test was ordered, it was time to tell my parents. I filled them in on almost everything, glad to have the chance to pull them out of the dark and by my side. Having them in the loop meant more phone calls, and strong suggestions to move back home. But I needed their love and emotional support, even if I had to constantly defend my need for independence.

#

My mother and I arrived at the hospital for my EEG. I had never walked through hospital doors alone. I imagined it would be a very lonely feeling. I was glad she was by my side.

The stale air conditioning escaped the building when the doors slid open. All hospitals smell the same: some kind of sterilizer mixed with air freshener covering sweat and fear and bodily fluids. This hospital felt more tomb-like than most, sealed and filled with artificial temperatures sinking to near-arctic levels. Cold buildings symbolize wealth in the desert. You had to be very poor or completely crazy to live without air conditioning.

I went in without any preparation or knowledge of what would happen. Without the Internet, I could not look it up and know what to expect, and no one had prepped me. I had no tools available to know if I received reasonable care. I could not look up EEG to dispel any uncertainty about what I might face walking into that hospital. I didn't even realize I was being tested for epilepsy. My mother waited while I went in.

The quiet, dark room did not feel like the rest of the over-lit hospital. It was small and had a gray metal machine with colorful wires, an examining table, and a single technician.

I do not remember many details about the first EEG, except the cool, sticky gel they globbed in my hair. I always had clean hair. If I didn't wash it, I thought about it all day. I remember the technician saturating electrodes to bury against my scalp, and then gently, adeptly positioning them in just the right places. I asked the tech what she saw, and she told me she couldn't say. Not because she didn't know, but because the hospital would not allow her to tell me anything. My doctor would contact me with the results.

I did not know until years later EEGs are approximately fifty percent accurate in diagnosing epilepsy. For months, doctors used this single unsuccessful test as evidence against me. They told me this EEG proved I did not have a physical disorder, while knowing the test was inaccurate half of the time.

#

Despite my increasing episodes, I continued to maintain a healthy social life, partially because I hated staying home alone. One evening I convinced Laurie, a friend from work, to check out line dancing and take advantage of a great happy hour at one of the local urban cowboy bars. The music was louder than country should be, and I was ready to leave shortly after we arrived.

A country bar is a strange place to meet a man from Germany. Henning did not belong there, and I did not belong there, but he had a friend, and I had a friend, and they found each other.

Henning wore a small, ironic smile, and spoke in a low, soft, heavily-accented voice. He worked for the military, doing something he couldn't tell me about. He had no roots in Tucson, and no desire to plant any. I needed him at that moment in my life.

He saw what was happening to me at night. It was far worse than what my brother saw in the hotel room in Colorado. I didn't want anyone to know, and Henning was good at keeping secrets.

I would not tell my parents my episodes were well documented by a man who slept with me. They liked imagining me alone in bed, and I did not want to take that away from them.

#

To my next appointment with my neurologist that June, he had me bring my parents. We were all worried the news would be devastating. Did he need them with me because he thought I

34

would be too upset to drive home? He had never met them, so asking for them to come surprised and confused all three of us.

I took solace in the fact that he had not called me right away, or scheduled a hurried appointment for me to come in. The EEG would have been read the day they gave it to me, weeks before. By the time this appointment came around, late June had arrived, with the clouds boiling up over the mountains. The summer monsoons sat perched on the desert's doorstep.

First he explained that my EEG was normal, as he had expected. He told us that ruled out epileptic seizures, which I had never even considered. What he concluded I had could not be determined by any kind of medical test.

My parents were as horrified as I was when he announced I was suffering from separation anxiety. He carefully explained that my parents' attention was all I desired. I did not want to move to L.A. or Denver because I was afraid to leave them, afraid of their disapproval. He decided they were smothering me, and trying to control me. In response, in order to avoid displeasing them and facing life away from them, I either "imagined" or "self-induced" nocturnal seizures—a word not used to describe my "episodes" before that day. Simply put, I was either faking or lying.

I couldn't deny that I constantly fought my overprotective parents for my independence. I wasn't always totally successful, but I had not actually lived with my parents for more than a summer since I was seventeen. I spent a summer in Santa Barbara attending UCSB summer school, and a summer with a theater company in Vermont. Yet, according to this neurologist, my very existence revolved around being close to my mother and father. I was so desperate to not move away from them, I was willing to go to the ultimate extreme. I sought self-destruction in exchange for the focus they gave me, and I desired only the attention I received from them by pretending to have seizures. He told them they further enabled, even encouraged me to be dramatic, by perpetuating the idea I could be an actress or screenwriter.

I don't know which of us felt most offended by his diagnosis. My diplomatic father turned fierce. My mother seethed silently, her green eyes smoldering. I left confused, humiliated, and in tears. I said confidential things to him, trying to help him understand what I wanted to do with my life when he asked, and he turned it all around on my parents, scolding them and belittling me. Beyond that, I received nothing to help me end what he called seizures other than strict instructions to stop working so hard to get my parents' attention, and to look into some therapy.

I felt like a traitor, betraying my parents who were trying to take care of me and help me find answers. I had no idea I was not speaking to the neurologist in confidence. I was a grown woman, not a minor. I signed my own forms and kept my own appointments. Not everything I told my doctors was meant for my parents' ears. I wondered if he thought he was doing me a favor, telling them what he assumed I could not say to them myself. Or if he simply felt he called my bluff, and opened the curtain to reveal my lies.

In this man's eyes, I faked my pain for dramatic purposes. After all, that graduate program I wanted to go to in Denver was in theatre, and so was my degree. I clearly lived for the adoration of others. I acted.

With an unreliable test and a single conversation, the explanation for my strange episodes had moved from stress to psychosis. The words came straight from my own mouth—I told him I wanted to act, and that my parents didn't want me to move away. There was no taking them back, unsaying what I told him myself.

Although he did not, to my knowledge, possess a degree in neuropsychology, he pronounced his "mental illness" decree with solid conviction. He was a highly trained and respected neurologist. Who was I to disagree?

I was Katie Scarlett Taylor, twenty-three, Tucson, Arizona, and I was ready to fight to prove I was not crazy.

Chapter 6—The Fight Begins

Not many twenty-three-year-olds have an eighteen-year career in their pocket. Before the neurologist diagnosed me with separation anxiety, I never thought about how much time and energy I had put into my acting, even before I started second grade. Standing on stage just felt like going home. Even when I got paid, it was never a job, but a privilege. Until my separation anxiety diagnosis, I did not fully appreciate what performing meant to me, how I built my life around just one thing.

I always wanted to be on stage. I never wavered, except to go back and forth between dancer and actress. Of course I had the socially acceptable ideas all little girls did at that time, to be a teacher and a writer. With those jobs you could be a good mommy and wife, roles I was told I would unquestionably play at some point in my life. But those were always second careers, set aside to follow my life as a performer. I would be a dancer and then a teacher, or an actress and then a writer.

My love affair with the lights and costumes began at five, after my first ballet recital. I felt no fear, no hesitation. I owned it. I could have stayed on forever. At eight, I performed with a professional ballet company. I experienced the life of a real dancer, with real costumes and a real green room, with grownup women and men who danced every day. My path was, I thought, set. I swore I would never abandon the wooden floors and dimming house lights.

Now, at twenty-three, one of my greatest assets in acting was gone. I could always memorize a script in one or two read-throughs. At that point, I could not have memorized a script at all.

My seizures began to erode my way forward. The path I thought I could never be distracted from grew fences I could not climb. The curtains closed, and I could only be in the audience.

The doctor used my acting against me. He saw me as a young woman needing an audience. Obviously, he decided, I lived for attention. I needed to perform. I faked my "episodes." I was only acting.

Acting went from the love of my life to my humiliating secret. In the doctor's official opinion, my love of the stage became evidence of my selfish narcissism. Obviously, still in Tucson at twenty-three, the bright lights of Broadway were not calling for me. I suffered delusions of grandeur, overestimating my talent, and my parents played along to enable me.

The seeds of theater can grow anywhere. To escape the monotony of life and exist for a short time in another world appeals to almost all of us. To empathize is a singularly human emotion, and exercising empathy satisfies the soul. In a place where everything seems washed clean of color, hot and dry, escape becomes priceless. Tucson is a perfect place for theater. I might have eventually returned there and found my own version of success.

I never called myself an actor again. That door closed. For the first time in my life, I did not have a dream.

The most difficult thing about being misdiagnosed with a mental illness is the more you fight it, the crazier you seem. No one wants to hear they inflict pain on themselves. Someone mentally unstable would certainly refuse to accept that diagnosis. After all, if all I wanted was attention, I certainly wouldn't be able to get it now that I'd been shown to be a fraud. Of course insane people fight against their doctors, especially when no test could definitively show mental illness. How can you disprove what can't be proven?

No two brains are the same; no one could see how my brain worked inside and no one could understand exactly how I felt. Even others with the same neurological condition felt the effects differently. The good and the bad, they were mine and mine alone.

The first neurologist took an ample amount of time with me. He spent more time interviewing me than almost every other doctor I went to see. If I had been less honest with him, if I simply said I was researching graduate programs when he asked what I intended to do with my life, and I wanted to be an engineer, I suspect my diagnosis would have been completely different. I asked myself, if my doctor had simply read about my symptoms in a book, without knowing my gender, would separation anxiety jump up at him?

Having a well-respected doctor can be a blessing and a curse. The neurologist who decided I had a psychological disorder had the respect of all the other doctors in town. Going to one of the best meant accepting his misdiagnosis. I found out the few minutes any doctor was willing to grant me would be prejudiced by the shining reputation of that first fallible, imperfect man with coveted degrees on his wall. My word did not stand up to his. For the next several months, I stood up to be pushed back down, one doctor after another.

ACT II:

LIGHTNING STRIKES

Falling down is not failure.
Failure comes when you stay
where you have fallen.

~ Socrates, philosopher, teacher, epileptic

Chapter 7—A New Normal

The July wind of cicadas buzzing through the desert air sounded like an oven timer, letting everyone know the ground was done baking. The monsoon clouds began turning heavy, filling with excitement, a short charge dancing white fire behind the shadows of gray promises. I would spend another summer in the desert.

Kim went on to Denver without me. I planned to catch up with her as soon as I had my episodes figured out. I lost one of my closest friends when she left.

As the summer stretched forward, a new concept faced me. Could doctors be wrong? Stress seemed an adequate first guess. But I was not making my seizures up to get attention, or making them happen out of spite for myself.

The well-respected neurologist-turned-psychologist who diagnosed me with separation anxiety could not be right, and many considered him one of the very best neurologists in the whole state. If he gave me the wrong diagnosis, who could make it right?

The Internet, in the 1990's, was in its infancy. The availability of immeasurable masses of twenty-four/seven medical information had not yet changed healthcare. I could not look up my symptoms and find another possible cause. I could not look up EEGs and learn they had a fifty percent success rate. I could not find testimonies from other patients, searching for the same answers. As far as I knew, I had been tested for epilepsy, and the test had been negative. I thought that was taken off the table as a possible explanation, and my doctors did nothing to dispel my certainty. So what else was there, beyond psychosis? No virtual medical source awaited my late-night searching.

I tried to focus on the waking part of my life, and to ignore my nights. Whatever it was, it only happened while I was in bed asleep, so it was not something that could kill me. I just had to wait for it to end, like a cold or stomach flu. The seizures began so suddenly, why wouldn't they end suddenly, too?

I fought to seem normal to everyone. I went about my days as if nothing worried me. I became an imposter in my own life, pretending to be myself, joking with coworkers, cheerfully chatting with my mother on the phone during her daily calls, telling her I was much better, making sure she couldn't sense my distress. No need to have her lurking around my apartment every night, watching me while I slept.

Privately, I examined every bite of food I ate, every soap and beauty product I used, my hair drier and furniture. Could an allergy be causing my whatever-it-was? Maybe the air in my apartment had toxins. Should I ask my neighbors if they had the same problems? Or contact the leasing office? I often caught myself staring at the wall, or at the ceiling, or at the clock, exhausted, contemplating all the possible and impossible, answers.

I never wondered if the diagnosis of separation anxiety held merit. Yes, I allowed my relationship with my parents to hold me back in some ways. But I was able to take full responsibility for my unwillingness to sever ties with them. I told myself I would eventually get out of Tucson, and they would learn to accept that I needed to be somewhere else to realize my dreams. I did not have anxiety. I simply did not have enough income. My problems were financial and physical, not emotional. I needed to figure out how to pay for my move, and where to find a job when I got to Colorado. My parents were not likely to help me, as they did when I stayed close to home where I could work for my father.

I knew I had lived a very sheltered life. My parents refused to let me have a job in high school because they didn't want me to be out by myself after dark. I'd never gone out and gotten a job anywhere other than the theater. The only "real" work I'd done centered around the family business. Even that became too much for me to manage.

The legendary heat in Tucson never disappoints. I continued to work for my father, not as a receptionist, but on a project-basis. Dealing with sleepless nights made me a zombie during the day, and freelance hours worked better for me than the strict time constraints that come with being the person who picks up the phones when the office opens. But July brought a desire for air-conditioned refuge, and leaving early for work became self-preserving. On most days I arrived at the office almost on time and left when I became too tired to continue.

#

The blazing 8:00 a.m. sun blanched the concrete stairs to my apartment, transforming them into glowing rectangles. Dizzy and unstable, I needed the metal railing to navigate them, regardless of the heat against my hand. I hurried across the parking lot in my pumps, feet already sweating in my pantyhose. I cursed July in the desert as even hotter air swam out at me while I climbed into the driver's seat. Not being diagnosed with "real" seizures meant no thought of giving up my license.

The project I worked on that summer changed my life. I learned to work in P.R., and I learned about the importance of reading. The "Read With Your Child" public-service campaign I helped my father create for one of his clients enjoyed great success and became a launch pad into my love for teaching children to read, which extended far ahead from what I could see in 1990. At that point in my life, I did not think about anything beyond the coming week.

The desert monsoons raced through our afternoons, delivering most of the precipitation our desert needed to thrive throughout the year. Booming symphonies of thunder accompanied spectacular lightning storms fracturing the sky, seeming somehow familiar to the storms in my head.

As dry arroyos became raging rivers and saguaros swelled with rainwater, my seizures increased in frequency and severity. I pushed ahead, trying to be the same to everyone, instead of the

45

stranger I became to myself. I lived my life day to day, feeling the world pass me by like the storms that made summer bearable. The effort to get out of bed, to remember what to do next, to speak clearly despite my gnawed, swollen tongue, took all of my diminished energy.

Henning stayed despite my worsening seizures. Whenever he went out of town for work, I would find reasons to visit my parents and stay the night with them. I did not want to lose my apartment or myself, but I knew I could not be alone. I found no humor in the irony that I really did begin to need my parents' attention.

One night, while staying at their house, I had to explain why I wore mittens to bed to keep from scratching myself. I told them the long scratches I used to find on my stomach and arms had disappeared when I started covering my hands, so I needed to wear the mittens to protect myself at night.

In the middle of the night they heard me moaning from the other room and rushed in to see me in the midst of a full tonic-clonic seizure. The seizure lasted about five minutes, with a thirty-minute postictal period during which I appeared disoriented and confused, not recognizing them or my surroundings. They finally saw what I hid from them for months, and I finally found out what Henning hid from me. He hadn't described in detail to me how severe my episodes had become. He probably thought I already knew.

\#

I tried to scream. Like the painting by Edvard Munch, when a blanket of electricity began to cover me, I felt distorted and hideous, my mouth open, trying to force noise from the deepest reaches of my soul, but no sound coming out. If only I could call out, I felt I could wake up and the seizure would stop. Instinctively, although I knew nothing would be accomplished, I tried shrieking at the top of my oxygen-deprived lungs, while my brain tried valiantly to suffocate me. At that point, four people had witnessed my seizures and told me I didn't make any noise other than gurgling and struggling for breath.

I knew seeing me have seizures terrified my parents. I hated scaring them. Coming back from what felt like "under," I could hear my mother's voice, stern, commanding, frightened. Telling me it was over. Asking if I was hurt, even though she knew I could not answer. Telling me to wake up, even though I was already awake. Never asking if I was okay because she knew I wasn't. I could hear my father talking to my mother rather than to me. Rushing to get anything he could think of, anything she asked for. Getting me glasses of water he knew I couldn't drink, but just needing to do something. Gently patting my leg while he waited, sometimes thirty, or even forty-five minutes, for me to come back. Wanting it to be better. Wanting me to be better. Me wanting to tell them "I'm fine," to tell them to go away and just leave me, to let me sleep, but not being able to communicate with them. Humiliating.

Immediately after a seizure, I could hear them and see them, but I could not communicate with them. I could hear myself breathing, sucking in as much air as possible through teeth I could not unclench, not being able to move my head off the puddle of my saliva that covered my pillow, which my mom would wipe gently from my face with what felt like pity. I wanted to push her away and tell her to stop, but my body did not listen to my brain. We would all three wait, silent and exhausted, until my breathing became normal. I would drink some of the water my father handed me, and my mother would change my pillowcase. I would eventually convince them to go back to bed and let me fall back to sleep. I was always so tired.

Chapter 8—The One

After six months, living day-to-day became enough of a challenge for me, and took all of my energy. My father began tugging on every string he could find. Finally, he convinced my physician to get me in to see another neurologist on "the list."

Because the neurologist I first visited commanded so much respect and influence in Tucson, most neurologists did not care to waste their time with me. They told us that patients, especially young women, often refused to immediately accept the diagnosis I had been given. But there was still one neurologist who ranked above my first neurologist in notoriety and respect. He could change my diagnosis and all would hail his genius.

This neurologist was the head of the hospital, the chief of the HMO, ranked one of the top doctors in the state, and nearly impossible to see. As a personal favor to my physician who could no longer avoid my father's bombardment, he agreed to see me.

The first neurologist had misdiagnosed me. I knew he was wrong. But this neurologist was better. He would certainly set it all straight. I still had some faith in doctors. I just needed another chance—a second opinion. I thought I had been through the worst of the neurologists. I could not have been more wrong. My few minutes with the second neurologist changed the way I will perceive doctors for the rest of my life.

I waited two months, from August until October, for an appointment, my seizures piling on me and ripping apart my brain. By the time my appointment came, summer retired, finally relenting to the greater distance from the Earth to the sun and the shorter days of fall. Desert colors become ordinary tans and khakis. No dramatic fall colors, or fall temperatures. The perfect weather every day began to draw the snowbirds back as each beautiful day resembled the last.

Henning was transferred out of town. There was not enough between us to last over distance. We spoke on the phone now and then, and I encouraged him to give his ex-girlfriend, who truly loved him, another chance. He did.

My ten-month lease expired at the beginning of October. I moved back to my parent's house, unsure of where I would live, still somehow hopeful about moving to Denver.

Living back in my childhood home, in my old bedroom, felt like a setback in my steadfast quest to prove my independence, and to show the doctors their assessment of me was false. I fought the need I had for my parents because the closer I moved toward them, the more plausible the separation anxiety diagnosis became. The hard truth was I needed help from someone, and they were always there.

#

My mother took me to my appointment with the top neurologist in Tucson because I could not remember anything. I was easily confused and could not risk misunderstanding any of his questions or answers. We knew we had to make the very best of the minutes we had been assigned to spend in his presence.

My mother sat in the chair next to mine. We both faced his big desk, waiting, the last of our hopes for answers spread like silent prayers across the dark wood.

The doctor finally made his entrance. He opened the door and stepped inside, smiling. He fixed his gaze on me.

"So. Who are you that you think you are so important that I should see you?"

I heard my mother take in a sharp breath, too stunned to respond to the sadist grinning at us. I faltered. Under his glare, I could not find the answer. I knew he thought he was being clever, but I really did not know how he expected me to answer who I was. I was tired and bruised and could not talk very clearly because my tongue and cheeks were chewed, bites all the way through on both sides. My head hurt so badly I did not even know I had a headache, because I had forgotten what it felt like not to have one. Was that the answer he expected?

"Katie Taylor," I finally managed to say, the sound of my voice and the look on my mother's face making me want to cry. I resisted because I knew, with my medical record saying I thrived on attention, tears were my dire enemy.

The neurologist shook our hands and sat behind his too-large desk, looking like a child wanting to play teacher. We watched him glance over my medical records, turning the pages too dramatically. He obviously had not seen them before, although we waited months for his help.

"And this is your mother?" he asked, his eyes still focused on my records. I hated it when someone referred to a person sitting right in front of them in the third person.

"Yes." I tried not to slur my "s." I always sounded drunk, so I used as few words as possible.

"Hmmm...." He glanced at me, and raised his eyebrows. He had obviously reached the "Separation Anxiety" paragraph. He didn't know how hard it was for an independent young woman to have to be taken places. I knew having my mother there would play into the first doctor's separation anxiety diagnosis, but I had no choice except to bring someone, and the best someone to bring was my mother.

"You've been to see my colleague."

"Yes."

"Hmm." He nodded.

I looked away, but my mother calmly returned his gaze when he looked at her. She took over the conversation from there. I do not recall what was said.

Somehow, we left after less than ten minutes with a referral to a neuropsychologist, some drug pamphlets, and a prescription for my first anti-seizure medication, Dilantin. I filled the prescription immediately and took the recommended dose. I spent two days unable to function.

All the time lost waiting for an opportunity to be granted an audience with "The One" ended in a failed prescription and a humiliating affirmation of my mental illness diagnosis. *No one will believe me now*, I thought.

#

My only hope for help became therapy. Maybe a therapist would tell them I wasn't crazy.

I made a visit to the neuropsychologist referred by the neurologist. I managed to get in to see him immediately after I called. A referral from the top neurologist in Tucson was undoubtedly a compliment for him.

The neuropsychologist generally thrived off of patients referred by the neurologists he worked with, or more accurately, worked for. His was not a specialty patients sought out without first seeing a neurologist, or two. Apparently, pleasing the bosses ranked high on this neuropsychologist's list.

For me, part of the attraction of psychotherapy was the knowledge that we all see the world differently. I had a certain desire to be told how unexpectedly unique and brilliant and complicated my brain was. Beyond that, I couldn't imagine how this man would change or help me. I did not expect him to change my seizures.

The appointment was long. For some reason I picture myself sitting on the floor, although that seems bizarre and wrong. I remember looking at Rorschach cards and trying to find meaningful ways to describe them. I remember crying. In the end, he told me he would contact my neurologist with his assessment, and he suggested I make an appointment to come back.

Why, I wondered, would his assessment go to the neurologist, and which neurologist? I had technically only seen each of them once. It seemed someone trained in psychology would be better qualified to recognize mental illness than a doctor of neurology. I thought that was why I went to see him, to refute the diagnosis I was handed and get confirmation of my emotional and mental normalcy. Did he work for the neurologist? I thought he had a separate profession and practice.

Unfortunately, this first psychologist placed his need to impress the doctors sending him referrals above the health of his patients. He existed to reassert the neurologists' diagnoses, not to make determinations of his own. He did not concern himself with helping me.

I did not make an appointment to return, and I did not get the trophy for most interesting patient I hoped for. Disappointment reigned. I would find someone else.

#

The second psychologist I sought out for treatment came recommended by a family friend. He had a very different assessment from my first doctor who shared his field. His advice to me was simple. I could schedule visits with him as often as I felt I needed to, but there was nothing psychologically wrong with me. I did not have separation anxiety. My seizures had some other yet-to-be-discovered cause.

This second doctor took a few significant things into consideration.

First my sleep deprivation. At that point I was experiencing frequent sleep-interrupting seizures. The amount, and quality, of my sleep were deeply impacted. Sleep is vital to everything cognitive, including memory, mood, and yes, anxiety. I didn't just go a night or two without sleep. I went three nights, four nights, sometimes more, waking several times, often unable to go back to sleep. I was a mental disaster.

Second, the uncertainty of my future. My life was thoroughly disassembled. If you can remember the feeling of not studying for a test, or sleeping through your alarm, or being stuck in traffic on your way to an interview, then you have experienced a fraction of the hesitation injected into my life.

Third, the effects of the seizures themselves. Regardless of their root cause, my seizures were mind-altering events. They were also physically painful. I felt indescribable dread when crawling into bed every night.

Being called sane by a doctor trained to treat mental illness gave me new direction. I never doubted myself, and now I had a medical professional solidly in my corner.

Chapter 9—Grace

In November, my birthday came and went, then Thanksgiving. Sweaters were unpacked. Turkeys were cooked.

My father remembers standing at his desk when he got the call from our family physician, who had first told me I simply had stress. I ran into him when I went to his office to see his nurse practitioner to get treatment for something. For the first time, he saw how the months of seizures had transformed me. My doctor told my father he was unhappy with my diagnosis. He wanted me to have another EEG, and an MRI.

Eleven months after my seizures began, I was finally given a referral to schedule my first MRI, and my second EEG.

First, I had my MRI. My mother seemed more nervous than necessary. She hated confined spaces, and she suffered serious sympathy pains for me. I didn't mind the test. Lying on a table, slowly entering a white tube, closing my eyes and pretending I was somewhere else, breathing in, breathing out, not thinking about anything. I managed to stay awake and relaxed during the test, despite the loud clanking and clicking noises the machine makes. Thankfully, the test showed nothing unusual.

Everything now hung on the second EEG.

#

I don't have a mind built for linear algebraic math, but I do see the world in patterns. I count. I measure. If there is a step that's about an inch deeper than the others going up a set of stairs, I have to step on it with my right foot. If I'm eating something that comes in pieces, say, candies or nuts, I have to chew the same number on one side of my mouth as I do on the other, so I can only take even numbers. When I'm walking down a sidewalk, I have to always step over the cracks with whatever foot first stepped over one. I do not know why, but I just have to.

While I sat with my parents on the roughly upholstered chairs in the hospital's waiting room, my father asked, "How many stairs?" and nodded his head toward the steps we climbed into that wing of the building.

"Four." We smiled.

"Yep," he answered.

He counted, too.

I went into the room by myself, and the technician seemed familiar. Maybe she was the same one I saw for my first EEG. I didn't ask her because I did not care one way or the other. I didn't care about anything. I just wanted to sleep.

She squeezed the clear gel onto the electrodes, and again I began to think about how dirty my wild hair would be after the test. I no longer brushed it, preferring to leave it long and tangled. The desert air-dried it in minutes in any season, regardless of smoothness, making blow drying irrelevant. My mother always complained and tried to convince me I would be much more attractive if I would use a hairbrush. She bought them for me, just in case I changed my mind and decided to be pretty. I had a drawer crammed with hairbrushes. At that point, I did not give a crap what I looked like.

I tried to transcend the moment, to surrender to the test. I had to be someone else—someone who was fine without clean hair. In that moment, I realized I had already become that person. I was someone totally different than the person who had an EEG in that room possibly with that woman six months before. And that was okay.

The moment when I decided to let someone fill my hair with jelly without caring whether or not my hair was clean, I transcended for the first to what I think of now as a state of grace, from "Why me?" to "I'm me. This is my journey. This is who I am." I sensed immediately that self-acceptance would come with great power.

While I felt the technician bury the electrodes on my scalp, I realized I had to save my fight for days when I needed it. Not for jelly in my hair. Not in the MRI tube. Not after a seizure. Fighting those things only meant beating up myself.

Tears of relief began to stream down my face. The tech stopped, concerned. "Are you okay? Is this hurting you?" I'm sure no one had ever been hurt by having gooey hair. She probably did not deal with many tears.

"I'm fine." And I was. I felt a calm I'd seen in others facing disease and loss that I'd never understood. A whisper in their ear, an un-furrowed brow. I needed to save my fight and prayers for when I needed them more. I needed to find moments of serenity when I could let go.

I don't know why my spiritual journey toward healing began in that dark little room. Afterward, in my life, little moments I felt were from a greater power came in strange and unexpected places. When meaning eluded me, when I could not see what happened inside me, or why it happened, everything could have been an answer, or at least a clue. A bluebird on a fence might be a sign of hope. A dream could be a visit from the mysterious decider who put us here—who put me here. Not my siblings, not my friends. Just me.

I had my waking EEG first, then my sleeping EEG to measure my sleeping brainwaves. I never imagined I could lie down and fall asleep in the middle of the day with wires snaking out of my head, but suddenly they woke me to tell me it was over.

I had an epileptic seizure during the EEG. The results were undeniable. I was not crazy.

Chapter 10—Endings and Beginnings

Christmas in the desert looks like a silly greeting card. Light strings weave through the thorns on cacti and Santa wears sunglasses, while his reindeer pull his sleigh through sand. Inside my parents' house, Christmas was traditional, beautiful, and magical. That first holiday since my seizures began, everyone could clearly see I had become a different person. My memory pains became sharper.

The family table always hummed with tales from the past. I could have been listening to strangers because I did not recognize any of the views from the open windows into our family story.

Someone mentioned a trip to Bermuda.

"We went to Bermuda?!" I blurted. A table full of surprised faces turned to me.

"You really don't remember?" asked my brother.

I felt like crying for a second, but I couldn't. Everything at the table was too beautiful and too familiar to me to be sad. I could still recognize the decorations pulled out every year of my life. The white nativity scene sat where it always had, and the stockings by the fireplace never changed. I laughed instead of cried. "Nope. Was it fun?"

They began to tell me about how badly I navigated the island on a bicycle, almost running into everything.

"You really don't remember that?" my sister asked.

"No." I began to see myself as they truly saw me. They described a goofy dodo I didn't know.

I sat at the table as a guest. I think my family began to realize how disconnected I felt. I could not defend myself against their versions of me. I couldn't say, "That wasn't me—it was Nancy!" or, "Yeah, but it started when you threw the rock at me!" I had no perspective to offer. Now it was only their family story.

#

After Christmas and before the new year of 1991 began, the second neurologist delivered the results of my EEG. I did not have to wait long to find a place on his appointment calendar this time around. When my mother and I got to his office, we waited, and waited, for over an hour before he barged in, this time wearing scrubs under his white coat, his eyes fixed on my results. I wanted to see remorse, to hear an apology for what I'd been suffering since he and his colleague got my diagnosis so wrong. The shadow of doubt, the hint of disappointment I wanted to witness didn't exist in this doctor's version of neurology.

Even with my EEG results in his hand, he hesitated to concede he had been wrong. Perhaps, he was forced to admit, I had a seizure disorder along with whatever emotional issues I had. He chastised me for not taking the Dilantin he had prescribed at our first visit. I told him I took one dose and could not stand up. I was so dizzy I could not walk to the bathroom without help. I felt nauseous and thought my head would split open from the pain it caused. I could not function on my own after the first pill. My mother corroborated my account. He told me I would have to find a drug to control my epilepsy and prescribed Tegretol instead.

I heard him say the word epilepsy, and realized for the first time what I had could not be cured. Somehow, I had been happy about being officially diagnosed with a brain disease because it meant I wasn't crazy. I hadn't grasped that everything I hoped for in my future might be completely unattainable.

I was Katie Scarlett Taylor, twenty-four, living in Tucson, Arizona, and I had epilepsy.

My new lifelong struggle began.

ACT III:

ARROYOS FLOOD

No man ever got very high
by pulling other people down...

~ Alfred Lord Tennyson, poet and epileptic

Chapter 11—The Girl in the Yellow Sweatsuit

The first time I saw a person have a seizure was in art class in first or second grade. It made enough of an impression that I actually remember details.

We were drawing self-portraits and then painting them. Mine still hangs in my father's office, long brown hair and eyes that looked like angry blue tires with black hubcaps on either side of the triangle nose. I remember I couldn't mix the paint to match the true color of my gray-green-blue eyes—they were too green, then too gray, so I just used straight blue. Not what I wanted at all. I was brooding about this when the little girl with dark, short hair and a bright yellow sweatsuit came into the portable classroom, late for some reason.

Classrooms always have one boy willing to risk everything to make the class laugh. This stereotypical boy from our class took advantage of the teacher not watching by pulling the little dark-haired girl's chair out a little too far so she missed the seat when she tried to sit in her place, probably a trick he learned from his several older siblings.

I looked when everyone started laughing, seeing her going down. Then kids were standing in a crowd around her, the teacher telling everyone to stand back. We could feel fear and uncertainty in his too-loud voice, and we huddled behind him like little cubs. The room was the quietest it had ever been. Everyone felt relieved they had not been the one who touched her chair, and the tough boy stood silently wiping tears. I was the smallest person in the class so I only saw the color yellow on the floor, and the backs of my classmates' heads. But the spectacle was enough to burn a place in my memory.

Later, we all learned the new word "Epilepsy", and were told never to mention the incident to the girl in the yellow sweatshirt and matching pants with elastic in the waist and ankles because she would not remember and would only be embarrassed. So no one ever spoke to her again. That was the easiest way to be certain we would never mention what had happened.

I wonder about her now, if she knew why she was isolated, or why she suddenly found herself in the hospital when she had been in art class moments before, or what medication she takes now or whether she is still alive. I wonder if she can drive a car, or if she has been choked or had her teeth knocked out by well-meaning people with outdated ideas trying to force something into her mouth to keep her from biting her tongue. Did her seizures stop when she got older? Without knowing her name, I will never know her story.

#

I had my diagnosis. I fought so hard to be something other than crazy. But now I had a devastating neurological condition to manage.

Epilepsy, to me, resided in all the stigmas where it lives on in others without the disease. My ignorance and misconceptions forced me toward categories I had never considered places for myself. Was I going to eventually end up in a vegetative state? Would I forever lose the ability to drive a car? Would others pity me, and avoid me, as we had avoided the girl in yellow? Or were the doctors wrong again? Was it really *epilepsy*?

I did not want to accept that like all epileptics' brains, mine was wired differently. Sometimes my brain emitted too much electricity and caused my body to seize. This might last for seconds or for hours, depending on the type of seizure. My brain betrayed me, and the damage seizures inflicted on my memory would last forever. How bad could it get? What would I become? How long could I be a mostly normally functioning adult?

Doctors expected me to instantly believe I developed a brain disease without explanation or apparent cause. My trust in neurologists eroded, and my fight against them landed me in an unkind landscape. I needed to figure out how to survive.

Chapter 12—A New Year

I began 1991 with an uncomfortable new title: Epileptic. Why me, when everyone else in my family had perfectly normal brains? I became an island.

My memory continued to deteriorate with every seizure, and my exhausted mind and body begged for respite. I had to pursue drug therapy. Like the first drug I tried, Dilantin, I reacted horribly to the Tegretol. I would not return to the asinine doctor who prescribed it, no matter how important or wonderful everyone thought he was. But when I asked my physician for another referral, no other neurologist from my HMO would see me. I had to travel off their list.

(I am extremely grateful my parents had the means to allow me to see a doctor not covered by our insurance. Many people struggle with medical bills. Over half of bankruptcies in our country stem from medical debt, which often is the first step toward homelessness. People who do what they must to survive cannot always first consider the cost. They end up owing more than they can possibly pay in a lifetime. I would have been in that boat.)

I also changed my general practitioner. My family's long-time physician seemed too intertwined with the debacle of my fight for diagnosis. I did not trust him.

January started well. I found an amazing apartment. I traded the three-story concrete block with concrete stairs for a 40's-era craftsman-style complex. The wooden buildings were only two stories. Thirty-two units, kept in prime condition, spread out around a large grassy common area. I had hardwood floors, no dishwasher, my first gas stove, and huge windows looking out onto the beautifully kept grounds with old-growth trees. I had a balcony for plants. I found a peaceful place I belonged, which I needed. I craved quiet, for my mind and my soul. The fact my apartment had no air conditioning did not really play a part in my decision, renting in January. It did have an evaporative cooler—that was the same thing, right?

I also got a border collie puppy I named Maggie. She gave me something to concentrate on, and something more to take care of than myself. She bounced around my life with joy and around my apartment with reckless abandon. Anyone can tell you border collies are not good apartment dogs. In fact, everyone did tell me that. Luckily my parents had a large yard and eventually adopted her from me.

That January I finally found a good neurologist. He listened and acknowledged the difficulties I suffered without judgment. He read my EEG and confirmed my diagnosis of epilepsy, dropping the separation anxiety like a smelly, wet sock.

He insisted I take medication. I explained why I was firmly against drug therapy. The inability to function during the day was far worse for me than the seizures at night, even though I sometimes had more than twenty seizures every week. There had to be another way.

He assured me there was not anything else he could do for me, which was true. Drugs were all they had to offer. Of course, my neurologist insisted I needed them—controlling my seizures was his job. I explained what I experienced with the other doctor's prescription for Dilantin.

"Are you sure?"

"Sure I couldn't even walk, or form a sentence?"

"No. Sure that was the dosage."

"Yes."

This doctor shook his head disapprovingly. I sensed he disliked the other pompous, overrated neurologist. That helped my confidence in him immensely.

"I would not give that much of that medication to a linebacker, much less to someone your size and weight."

He did not actually say the words, but I knew he was telling me the other doctor over-prescribed the Dilantin. The tops of my ears burned and I felt my face go blank with anger. He suggested Tegretol, and I told him that had not worked for me, either.

"Why don't we try Tegretol again, and start with a low dose. It's a better drug. There are comparatively fewer side-effects."

Comparatively is a word I quickly came to associate with seizure medications.

There were not many drug options at that time: Dilantin, Tegretol, Depakote, and Phenobarbital. I eventually tried all of them, singularly and in combination with each other. I went through weakness, lethargy, and exhaustion. I gained weight. Medications changed me psychologically, as well, bringing mood changes and constantly deepening depression. My distant and near memories hid from me. I felt myself becoming a reluctant addict, beholden to drugs no one could enjoy.

#

"Can you still have babies?" was my grandmother's question.

People loved my grandmother. She was gregarious and modestly flirtatious with men and women in the way only a Southern belle can be. She taught me that people wanted to feel important, and that you catch more flies with honey than with vinegar. She gave me a copy of the book, *How to Win Friends and Influence People,* when I was sixteen and made me promise to read it. I don't remember if I ever did.

I do not deny I was my grandmother's favorite, and neither would she. I tried not to talk to her about my seizures because I feared she might question what I often asked myself: *What had I done to make God punish me with seizures?* Instead, she probably wondered why God punished her by choosing her favorite to curse with an embarrassing disease.

"I'm not interested in having babies."

"Not now—but someday."

"Yes, epileptics have babies."

She frowned. "I'm not talking about that." She disliked associating me with the word "epilepsy." "Some medicines make you unable to have babies. What about all the ones you are taking?"

I dragged the big medication bible off my parents' bookshelf and looked up the meds I'd tried. Some of the medications I tried caused infertility. Others I tried caused birth defects and other complications during pregnancy. No one had discussed any of the possible future harms I might face if or when I wanted a family.

I felt betrayed again by my doctors. Why didn't they tell me I might not have children? I never stopped to imagine what it meant to be a woman who never had a baby. I'd been told since I was a young girl, I would be somebody's wife and somebody's mommy and I'd be very happy. Who would ever consider a wife who couldn't have babies? Would I ever be able to love someone who didn't want children?

I couldn't take another thing making me eternally single. Medications were killing me.

#

The long, tall branches of the Ocotillo cacti lit up like birthday candles, red blazes at the end of every spindly arm. The colors of spring were back, and evaporative cooling, effective for about a three-foot radius, would take some getting used to. I did go through nights, sometimes even weeks, without seizures. My tongue had time to heal between rounds, and my mind felt clouded by drugs rather than electricity.

I frustrated my doctor by constantly skipping doses, or by adjusting dosages myself. We both knew my seizures occurred while I slept in a controlled environment, protected from the usual dangers epileptics face. I would not crash a car. I would not fall from a ladder or drown in a bathtub, unless I fell asleep. I didn't worry about things other people with my disease feared, and instead placed what he considered far too much importance on feeling like I used to before seizures.

This was not just my personal war waged against drugs and doctors. My parents had a big stake in the game. Sometimes they were on my side, and sometimes they were on the doctor's side. They desperately wanted me to find a drug therapy. I told them the basics about how bad I felt, but I never divulged the depth of my struggle. I loved my new apartment and needed my own space. They helped pay my rent, and I knew they could decide at any time to cut me off and move me back to their home.

I wanted to find some way to make myself better, normal, the exact person I was without the drugs. I wanted to write and make people laugh. I felt the drugs making me into someone I did not know and did not want to be. If I could just get rid of the drugs, I thought I could be me again.

As quickly as it arrives, spring moves on. Palo Verde trees, full of blooms one day, will empty them overnight, covering everything outside with a layer of soft, tiny yellow flowers. Desert creatures begin to stake out their scraps of shade.

I did not even consider the possibility of escaping Tucson before another summer began. I resigned myself to being a desert girl.

Chapter 13—Texas

Summer, as it always does, returned.

My mother searched relentlessly for answers. Through a friend in Houston, where my parents are from, she managed to arrange for me to participate in a sleep study at the Baylor University Hospital at the end of July.

When I told him I had an opportunity to visit an actual epilepsy clinic at Baylor University where I would be given an overnight EEG, my neurologist was encouraging and enthusiastic. In his letter to my physician:

The patient has raised the idea of obtaining an opinion at an epilepsy specialty clinic. I think at this point with all that she and her family have been through, that makes good sense.

Twenty-four hour EEG monitoring is common today. In 1991, not many places were set up to offer overnight testing. This was a fantastic opportunity.

My mother and I had a nice drive to Houston together. I remember staying overnight in San Antonio, enjoying their beautiful river walk, despite the July heat.

Texas heat is nothing like Tucson heat. The humidity keeps the nights as warm as the days. In Tucson, at least the evenings become bearable.

All the hype and excitement fell flat at the sleep clinic. I remember being hooked up yet again with EEG electrodes, being videotaped and being given something to help me sleep in a lighted room while wrapped with wires decorating me like a Maypole. Even though they took my medications away, I did not have seizures. The doctors were wonderful, and I received excellent care. But without actually having a seizure during the

69

monitoring, nothing significant could be recorded. My father flew out and met us in Houston, and we headed for home in a haze of disappointment.

My boyfriend at the time, Craig, was working in Texas, and met us in San Antonio, to ride home to Tucson with us for a visit. He took us to Sea World and we enjoyed a nice day there despite my parents' constant complaining about the heat, before setting out to make a quick visit to a campground where we often stayed when I was a kid.

My family spent months at a time at Garner State Park. I remembered loving it there, but specifics about the people and events I experienced as a child died somewhere during my seizures. Taking Craig would make me closer to him than anyone else in my life. By the end of the day, just by being there and seeing the physical objects I held in my memory, he would know almost as much about where I spent my childhood summers as I did.

My memories of Garner and the campground where we stayed—Cold Springs—ran through my mind like a slideshow, with a few quick snippets of scenic film mixed in. I mostly remembered sensations and bold images rather than actual people or events. I could look back and see a giant watermelon cooling in the spring box halfway down the long concrete stairs on the path to the river. I could see a perfect rock platform for jumping into the Rio Frio, the only thing cold outside of the icebox. I could see the clouds building, and rebuilding, and my siblings and cousins looking for clear spots through the rain. My mind held pictures of me slapping mosquitoes and fishing for catfish, tubing down the river, wearing shoes in the water to protect my feet, feeling the squishing of the soggy soles in the three-dollar tennies I got just for that summer, always red with white rubber trim. Inside my brain was a shot of my sister and me carrying the inner tubes we personalized with waterproof paint through the places too shallow to ride over without scraping our butts, then another shot taken after five or six hours, landing at the dance pavilion at Garner State Park. In the distance there was a knotted rope tied to a tree branch that if you didn't let go out over the water, they said you'd die getting smashed on the rocks. And an image of me washing a Moon Pie down with a Big Red soda bought from an old machine for a dime.

On the way to Garner from San Antonio, I can remember I didn't feel well. The sleep study exhausted me, and the hilly road from the back seat made me slightly nauseous. Beyond that, I have maybe two minutes' worth of memories for the rest of the day, into the night, and the following day. I only vaguely remember having seizures in the back seat of the car, then throwing up on the side of the road. The lack of medication for the sleep study caught up with me. Apparently I went into status epilepticus—my seizures piled on top of each other, one after another, with no recovery in between. I sank behind a curtain of absolute darkness.

Beginning the next day, I remember my mother softly calling my name, telling me I had some seizures and was in the hospital in San Antonio. I didn't care where I was. I didn't care about anything.

In that San Antonio hospital, I remember thinking, *I could give up, and no one would blame me. I could surrender to my seizures, let others take care of me for as long as I managed to live through them.* I wanted to stop striving. But I knew my friends and family would never give up, and I owed it to them to continue the fight.

#

We returned to Baylor for another night of study. I had three seizures and learned some frightening details about my epilepsy.

Yes, my seizures were nocturnal, and I was safely in bed, but they were not harmless. According to the readings in the sleep study, my oxygen level dropped to zero for up to two minutes during my seizures. I could be one of those patients who actually die from the disease.

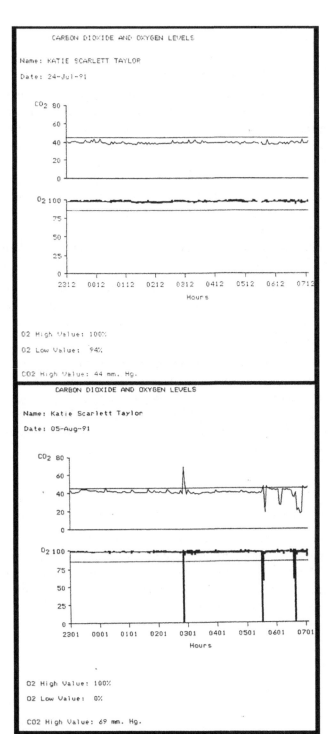

CARBON DIOXIDE AND OXYGEN LEVELS

Name: KATIE SCARLETT TAYLOR

Date: 24-Jul-91

CO_2 80

O2 High Value: 100%

O2 Low Value: 94%

CO2 High Value: 44 mm. Hg.

CARBON DIOXIDE AND OXYGEN LEVELS

Name: Katie Scarlett Taylor

Date: 05-Aug-91

O2 High Value: 100%

O2 Low Value: 0%

CO2 High Value: 69 mm. Hg.

72

If I had accepted the original misdiagnosis I received and opted for psychological care rather than the neurological care I forcefully pursed, I probably would not have survived.

#

Dr. Rutecki, the neurologist in Houston, sat on a rolling stool, like the first neurologist I had. While he talked, I stared at the instruments in this room where my EEG had been recorded. The room felt very small, and my head felt like a solid brick of marble after bouncing on and off my meds and the seizures I had over the days prior.

He was adamant. He told me firmly I must take drug therapy seriously. I had to live with the drug side effects, or I might not live at all. There was no other way. We went home and I started Tegretol with Depakote. I felt worse than ever.

After a short visit, Craig went back to Texas, and, like Henning, the distance proved too much for the strength of our connection. Having him see me at my lowest point, a moment I wanted to put behind me, made me want to sever ties. I turned him loose and jumped back into dating.

Chapter 14—Drug Wars

I didn't like the Depakote. I told my doctor I could not talk clearly or remember simple things. I felt angry, and depressed. I felt stupid and numb. He continued bouncing dosages around, trying to find some combination of drugs I could tolerate, with Tegretol always factored in.

I did not like Tegretol. I had been taking different dosages of it for over half a year. It made my memory complete mush and made me emotional. I would describe these side effects, and my doctor would tell me, "This drug doesn't do that. It's a good drug." I tried to make him understand it wasn't a good drug for me.

These were drugs that worked for other people. Tegretol was a game-changer for neurologists who had started their careers with nothing to offer but barbiturates. I was being non-compliant, not giving this breakthrough in treatment a good chance. I expected too much.

After you describe something dozens of times, each time to the same person who doesn't understand what you are telling him, you start to lose words. You start to feel like nobody understands you. You begin to question yourself. How could I make him understand that on Tegretol I could not remember anything—anything at all? What was my sister's name? Which apartment was mine? The mystery game that my life became was exhausting.

#

A hot wind whipped the dry air into a torturous blast. The smell of baked asphalt raped my senses. The shiny black street seemed liquid, grabbing at my flip-flops as I crossed to the neighborhood convenience store for a bag of ice. I held the bag of frozen blocks against my body on the walk back, the burning cold as unpleasant as the burning hot wrapping around my ankles. The rectangles turned to ovals before I crossed the street and traveled the short distance to my apartment. And I couldn't remember why I went to buy ice in the first place.

#

I so desperately wanted by mind back. And I wanted my life back. I decided to just take it back myself.

From my standpoint, the drugs were worse than the seizures. Even after Houston where I learned the danger I faced, I didn't want to trade my seizures for my ability to stay awake, or my ability to form a clear thought, or have friends and be fun. Why was death worse than a miserable life?

Epilepsy drained my mind, no doubt. But combining that with drugs was a double disaster for me.

When the days became perfect that fall, Kim came to visit from Chicago, where she lived after her year in Denver. We always laughed together. We cracked each other up. She knew me from college and was around at the beginning of my seizures. I didn't have to explain to her how I ended up here from where I came from. She knew I didn't remember things and didn't need to talk about the past. She lived where I always wanted to be— in the present.

When she came, I stopped taking my medication. I wanted to be able to laugh and talk like myself, instead of needing extra time to process conversation. I felt pretty well, so on her last day in Tucson, I made a very bad decision.

Combining medication withdrawal with Margarita happy hour at a restaurant walking distance from my house apparently ended in disaster. Or so I heard.

#

"Your name...? Your social-security number...? Your date of birth...?"

These were questions everyone knows the answers to—I knew that much. But I could not answer her. I was laughing because I really didn't know, but I didn't know what that meant, or what that was called when you don't know anything. Perhaps the Margaritas were to blame; alcohol had obviously affected me more than I expected, but I did not understand in that moment the gravity of having a daytime seizure. I sounded funny telling this woman I didn't know these things and so I laughed. She was annoyed.

"Do you know who this is?" she asked, leaning in to me and speaking loudly, as if that would help.

"Ahhhh, no!" I could see my friend, but I didn't know her name. But the nurse pointed at an older woman sitting next to me. She was pointing at my mother. I found out later that Kim called her when I started convulsing uncontrollably at the bar and then checked out.

My mother was pale, embarrassed and furious with her tequila-soaked daughter, while I could not even grasp the concept of mother. I could tell she was somebody really mad, but that just seemed funny, too, so I laughed again. My friend looked terrified, knowing my mother could explode any second. To me, it didn't matter who she was. I was untouchable in the hospital. I had nothing to fear from anyone.

I was in the hospital for a couple of days. My neurologist insisted I agree to give drug therapy a serious try before he would release me. I did not even remember that, until he reminded me later.

#

Back on Dilantin, I could not stay awake. I could not work. I went back to my dad's office for a while because he had a side office where I could sleep when I needed to. I went from never napping and only sleeping five hours a night, to only staying awake for five hours at a time. Everyone did their best to treat me normally, but I thought they all saw me as a charity case. Whenever I felt myself falling asleep sitting or standing up, I slipped into the quiet little room and curled up on the small couch to fall asleep in shame.

"You take naps? I never even noticed." When I finally talked to my friend Laurie from work about my insecurities, I learned a valuable lesson. Not everyone was thinking about me all the time. They lived their own lives and dealt with their own problems. They didn't care if I napped. Not everything was always about me.

#

I woke up in the middle of the day, asking myself in a panicked whisper how I could sleep at a time like this. I tried to jump off the bed without sitting on the edge first and tripped over the shoes waiting faithfully on the floor. Landing on my hands and knees, I took a deep breath to calm myself. It was too late to try to go to work today.

I sat back on the bed and watched a cricket move across the floor. Jones, my cat, hadn't seen him, and the cricket had no way of visualizing what a long, horrible death a cat could provide. I wondered if he would rather die quickly, beneath my fatal step. I thought about his crunchy exoskeleton under my bare foot—a last, quick jerk, a reflexive motion tickling the comparatively softer skin of my arch.

Jones saw the cricket and perched in anticipation. I lifted him out of the room and closed the door, stepping carefully around the bug. I fought the urge to move to the couch and lie back down, but I decided to go outside and sit on my balcony, visiting my plants instead.

My neurologist wanted me to see a new doctor and recommended a woman from another practice. I could understand why a patient who refuses to get well was difficult for a doctor to accept. I understood why my neurologist passed me along to another neurologist after he ran out of ideas and drugs to try. It was the right thing to do.

Chapter 15—Records

The first time I saw the next neurologist was in November, the day before my 25th birthday, two years after my seizures were diagnosed. When I went for my appointment, she had not looked at my file. She gave me dubious looks as I tried to explain my unusual case to her, and asked me several "Are you sure" questions. Yes, I was sure I was aware of my seizures, they only happened while sleeping, and they came in clusters. She asked me what meds I took and increased one, despite me telling her I came to her because the meds were causing debilitating side effects, and my other doctor was out of ideas. She assured me she would be all caught up on that the next time we met.

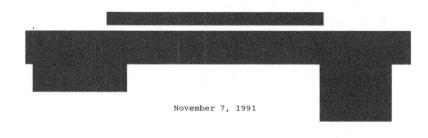

November 7, 1991

M.D.

RE: TAYLOR, KATIE S.
       Date of Birth: 11-08-66

Dear Dr. ███████:

Katie is seen today in follow-up of her seizure disorder.
She has had her medication increased to Tegretol 400 mg a
day and Phenobarb 90 mg per day.   In spite of the increase
she continues to have frequent small seizures as often as
three or four times a week.   She complains of tiredness
and fatigue on the higher doses of the medications and some
difficulty with memory.

EXAMINATION: Her examination is unchanged.

PLAN: I have asked for her to have drug levels today and
will speak to her tomorrow.   We will then decide about
further increasing her anticonvulsant dosage.

Sincerely,

M.D.

██:lk

Thanks to holiday hiring, I found a job I loved, selling clothes in my favorite boutique. The owners, Colleen and Maurice, proved to be two of the best bosses I have ever had. They were lovely to me, and I learned to work retail sales from the best in the business. I would use the skills they taught me throughout my life. I loved sales, and in my twenties and thirties, whenever I needed to find a job to carry me through a rough spot, retail had a place for me.

My new neurologist wanted my physician to order another MRI. He complained loudly about the expense, denying the

79

request initially. I did eventually get the order, and thankfully, the test was normal, again.

That December, my sister had her first son. Scott was born on my father's birthday, healthy and screaming as all babies should. Christmas was magical with a baby in the family. He became the light of our lives.

#

My new neurologist seemed thoroughly unengaged, and over that winter and spring in 1992 I became my own doctor. I decided several times to improve my life by not taking the drugs, or adjusting the doses. But the euphoria of being off meds and being able to remember how to do things, like turn on my stove, without an enormous amount of concentration and hesitation never lasted long. My brain always eventually reminded me why I had to take them. When my seizures overwhelmed me, coming in clusters of up to ten per night, destroying my tongue and the sides of my mouth, I would start the meds again, knowing a chemical castration of my creativity and concentration possibly prevented my death.

#

I woke up on the floor, unable to rearrange my contorted body. Thrown on the ground like a doll, I lacked the electrical ability to move my limbs. A pain grew on my side, like a deep throbbing, but I couldn't rearrange myself to ease the hurting. Burning anger forced a scream from my deepest reaches, but it merely gurgled out of me like a throaty moan, barely audible. I willed my arm off the floor telekinetically. It slapped me awkwardly, bending at the wrist where my fingers were frozen, claw-like. Breathe in, breathe out. Patience. I must be patient. I felt warm tears dripping off my face onto the hardwood. My throat tightened. I felt the depression, felt like going down the road to surrender, to self-pity. But I wouldn't. I could have easily given up. People would have understood. I could've let my parents take care of me. That's what most people would've done. I tried to tell myself, "That is what I should do." My breathing became more regular, and then the pain of my mouth being badly bitten again raised my anger for a moment, until I remembered the stabbing in my side. I was able to move my limbs awkwardly like a newborn deer, but every time I tried to straighten myself my breath was forced out by the pain in my side. I had no choice. I couldn't lie on the floor all night. With monumental effort I got on my hands and knees, then with the nightstand's help, just my knees. That was better. But every breath in was torturous. I sat on my bed, wanting to get back in, but the pain of sinking into the mattress put me back on the floor on my knees. I stood up, then sat, then lay back, but lying down felt like an anvil had been placed on my chest. I surrendered, and shuffled into the other room to perch on the edge of the couch, dozing on and off until the sun rose.

It's impossible to hide bruised ribs, especially if you are a hugger. Or if you sit, or lie down, or even if you breathe. No one was happy with my meds when I actually hurt myself. It was summer, again, and my mom decided it was time for another visit to the neurologist. When she wanted me to go, she became relentless. I eventually gave in.

In the waiting room, I stared at a poster on the wall of a child with big new teeth, smiling on a swing. Two things epileptic children dream of are teeth and swings.

They called me in. I waited. She finally came in. Seven months after I became her patient, she still had not looked at my medical records. She sent me for blood tests to check my medication levels and told me she'd call to tell me if I needed to increase my dosages.

I went there to tell her my meds were not working. My days were becoming worse than my nights. The side effects were unbearable. She didn't hear a word I said. She only prescribed.

I walked out of her office feeling more frustrated with doctors than I had felt in almost two years. I left that July appointment knowing I needed a new doctor, again. But I had no options left in Tucson. I would have to put up with her.

NEUROLOGICAL SURGERY

NEUROLOGY

July 1, 1992

M.D.

RE: TAYLOR, KATIE S.
     Date of Birth: 11/08/66

Dear Doctor ████████:

Katie is seen today in follow up of her nocturnal seizures.
She was last seen in November. She was doing well by her
definition, having seizures about once a week only at
night until about six weeks ago. She began having several
seizures a night. She has been under more stress because
of the new job, although she has had regular sleeping
habits and does not drink alcohol. She thinks that her
seizures can also sometimes be brought on by hot dogs,
chocolate and perhaps caffeine, as well as increasing
stress. She does describe some feelings of tiredness from
the medication. She also states that she has had a few
episodes of jerking or twitching of the left arm that
occur during the daytime.

EXAMINATION: Her examination is unremarkable.

Drug levels were done two weeks ago with a Tegretol of 4
and phenobarbital level of 15.

IMPRESSION: Katie is having increasing nocturnal seizures,
possibly stress related. She has low therapeutic levels
of both of her anticonvulsants.

PLAN: I have asked her to increase the Tegretol to
100 mg. in the morning, 150 mg. in the afternoon and
200 mg. at h.s. She may need increasing doses for better
seizure control. This has always been a problem because
of side effects. She is to call me in two weeks with a
progress report.

Sincerely yours,

M. D.

████:cd

*(During a neurological exam, doctors ask if you are right-
or left-handed. Although recently disputed, traditional research
showed a higher incidence of epilepsy in left-handed people. An
unusually high number of left-handed epileptics have no genetic
marker for their handedness—like me, they are usually the only
left-handed person in their family.)*

#

I avoided my neurologist after it became apparent that she had nothing new to offer. After a year of being her patient, she still had not looked at my records.

After three years, seizures simply forced themselves into the landscape of my life. I became more skillful at pretending I remembered things and acting like I knew things. I figured out how to introduce people I apparently knew to others so I could hear their names.

"Hi! How are you? This is my friend Liz from work."

Liz would put out her hand, and he would take it. "Hi, I'm Stuart."

Of course, that was it. Stuart. I could do the same to figure out who he was, and how I knew him. It was exhausting, but I didn't have to keep saying, "Sorry, but I have epilepsy, and... blah blah blah."

When I decided I could no longer live with the side effects of Tegretol, and my neurologist refused to try anything new, I had to search once more for a new perspective. Again through connections, my father arranged for me to see a neurologist at the Mayo Clinic in Scottsdale in December. I wanted to be sure this doctor actually looked at my medical records, but my Tucson doctor forgot to send them. When they told me there was no time for my records to be sent, I picked up a copy myself to take with me.

The thick packet was heavier than I expected. As I weighed it in my hands, I realized I had never actually seen my medical records. I decided to take a look, to make sure everything important was in there. I knew I probably only had one chance to see this doctor, so I didn't want anything to be left out.

When I read the letters passed behind my back like notes from mean girls, I felt stunned. At first, I wanted them out of my records, and I thought about removing them. But then I felt glad they were there. They were so shockingly unprofessional, any real doctor would find them offensive. These letters accurately represented the deplorable humans I had dealt with.

The letter with the most bite came from the neurologist supposed to be the best in Tucson. He for whatever reason wrote to my physician's partner, who I never met. He not only got my doctor wrong, he spelled my name wrong, and got my age and my handedness wrong.

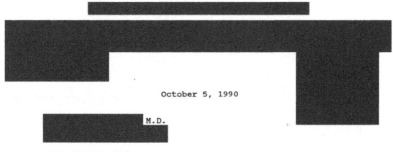

October 5, 1990

████ M.D.

RE: TAYLOR, Katy
    DOB: No Chart

Dear ████:

I saw Katy, needless to say she is a delightful young lady, 24 years of age. Her present complaint is of a choking feeling when she is asleep, where she can't breathe; then her family finds her with her arms up, her eyes rolled up and her legs stiff but she has an awareness of what is happening. She has had multiple episodes. She has had other episodes where her right leg jerks, also has had heaviness and pain in her head.

She was worked up for seizures by ████ and the inference that I got was that both you and ██ think she has big time psychological problems.

Needless to say her neurologic exam in total is normal.

I spent an enormous amount of time with Mother and daughter, and I finally got them to buy into the concept of psychiatric testing. I told her that I wasn't convinced whether it was a pure panic disorder or had some underlying affect disorder. She was willing to consider either one of these.

Thanks ████.  You owe me a brain tumor for this one!

I remain,

Respectfully,

████ M.D.

████/mmg/nc

84

In my ten minutes with him, he confirmed my diagnosis of having "big time psychological problems." I felt dizzy with embarrassment, knowing this letter, from the most respected neurologist in town, lingered in my medical records.

His second letter referred to the fact my father complained to our physician that my mother and I waited over an hour for our second appointment. He obviously did not, even with my new EEG in hand, easily change his first diagnosis.

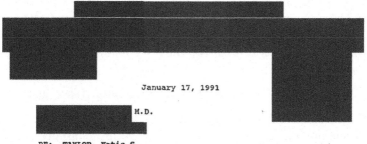

January 17, 1991

███ M.D.

RE: TAYLOR, Katie S.
     Date of Birth: 11-08-66

Dear ███:

Two things - one I was on time, and second I spent a great deal of time with Katie, in fact gave her things to read.

Prior to this I had reviewed her EEG at ███'s request.

I re-questioned her and I still have a little bit of misgivings even though her EEG is clearly abnormal and paroxysmal at this time, especially with the statement of saying with concentration I can stop some other things but the bottom line is I think one has to believe that there is probably now a seizure process going on with whatever else is on top of it.

She did not like the Dilantin; I frankly feel that I would try her on Tegretol. I gave her the VA combined study which she sat and read in my office, which describes the effects of Tegretol, Dilantin, Mysoline and Phenobarb in the treatment of seizures. After reading this she has agreed to a therapeutic trial on Tegretol. I fully explained to her that it really is a much safer drug than she imagined.

I explained to her about bruising or other side effects where she might call me immediately or stop the drug. I gave her a course getting up to two pills a day slowly over about a week, and a slip for blood tests.

I also rescheduled to see her in three weeks.

Thanks. I remain,

Respectfully,

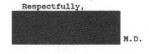

███ M.D.

███/mmg

(Lift your arms and put them out to your sides, like Davinci's Vitruvian Man. Touch your nose with your left hand, then with your right hand. Next, track a slow-moving object with your eyes, side to side, from one periphery to the other. Eyes forward, stand on your left foot, then on your right. Walk in a straight line, one foot in front of the other. Hold your arms out in front of you and resist the pressure of someone pressing down on one, and then the other. Did you pass your neurologic exam?

A neurologic exam takes approximately five to ten minutes. When seen in my medical records, it does not indicate an enormous amount of time spent between doctor and patient. No special equipment is required. The test could be performed in a busy parking lot.)

Next came the assessment from the neuropsychologist.

His three-page, single-spaced account of our one-hour discussion did admit the characteristics of my "episodes" were commonly indicative of partial seizures. He did not necessarily think I suffered from a big-time psychological problem, yet he was unwilling to contradict the diagnosis handed down to me.

"...In short, if it has been determined her "seizures" are psychogenic, several psychodynamic possible causes are evident. I would certainly defer to you and Dr. X regarding the significance of the episodes Ms. Taylor is reporting..."

It seemed to me that someone trained in psychology would be better qualified to recognize mental illness than a doctor of neurology. Unfortunately, this first psychologist placed his need to impress the doctors sending him referrals above the health of his patients.

I couldn't believe how many ways he twisted my words to satisfy the neurologist's diagnosis. I thought back to the strange, leading questions he asked, and the unnecessary directions he guided my answers. In his account, he did an excellent job of making me sound crazy.

As I read and reread the letters with horror, I realized I never actually had a second opinion. They all just echoed each other, each concurring with the original diagnosis without considering that a doctor—especially their friend and colleague—could've possibly been wrong. I thought about the months of my time wasted, the money wasted. My hope for a better answer, a second chance, had been futile. I should have known, based on the lack of time spent with me after waiting months for appointments, that they only regurgitated into my records what the first doctor decided. It went all the way back to that first peck on the cheek, that very first "It's just stress."

After reading their correspondence, my faith in doctors disintegrated into dust. I truly hated them.

#

Although he lived an adventurous life, my maternal grandfather never told stories about his past. He had a gift for living entirely in the present. And I would have sworn his hand gripped my shoulder that morning, waking me at six. He was always, perhaps a result of farm and military life, an early riser. His touch woke me from the seizure gripping my body, and I did not go back to sleep.

Instead I crawled into the shower, following the trail of footprints my cat left in the dust on the floor. I tried to remember important things I was supposed to do. Things like showers, which at that point couldn't be avoided, and doctor's appointments.

I studied the long strands of hair decorating the bottom of the tub when I finished and turned the water off, looking for some clue about what the day might hold as if they were tea leaves with some mysterious message hidden that only I could read. Nothing.

On to Phoenix, to see yet another neurologist.

#

The Mayo Clinic Scottsdale is an impressive hospital. I had not been anywhere like it before. Going there in December, 1992, changed my life.

The well-appointed office where I met Dr. Hirschorn did not have an examination table or cold florescent lighting. She looked at my records and seemed unaffected by the outrageous musings of my former neurologists she most certainly knew by reputation, if not personally. She told me the tests I had clearly, unmistakably showed I had epilepsy, just like fifty million other people in the world. It wasn't an unusual or complicated diagnosis. She also did something no doctor had done before— she listened without prejudice. Regardless of what other neurologists wrote about me, at that moment I was her patient, not theirs.

At that time, surgery had become an option, but it was ordinarily reserved for people with debilitating daytime seizures. Yet, with the number and frequency of my seizures, and the lack of oxygen they enforced, she said she didn't think I should rule it out as an option if drugs continued to prove so difficult for me to tolerate.

She offered to continue as my doctor, but told me the best thing for me would be to find someone in Tucson to take over. She referred me to a neurologist at the University of Arizona who was quickly becoming a force in treatment for epilepsy. She assured me he was different from the other neurologists I'd seen, and that he was actively searching for new ways to help people with my disease.

In one appointment, she changed my life. Not because of anything she did to me, but because she affirmed my need to be considered mentally sound, and she acknowledged that medication was a serious problem for me that was hindering my quality of life, and that was a bad thing. However, the most important thing she did was send me to someone else. She referred me to the doctor who would save my life.

I was Katie Scarlett Taylor, twenty-six, Tucson, Arizona, and after nearly four years, I finally found a neurologist who would listen to me.

Chapter 16—A Real Doctor

When I was a child, my pediatrician was one of my favorite people in the whole world. He had enormous hands and breathed through his mouth when he listened to my insides working with his cold stethoscope. He hummed. He removed my tonsils. I liked Dr. Eberling so much I convinced my mother to take me into his office at the start of any slight medical symptoms. He called me Sarah Burnhardt, a famous actress from his youth.

Of course he knew my talent for exaggeration and fully supported my decision to become an actress someday. But he never told me I was just stressed, or only imagining I had a fever or stomachache. He was a caregiver, not a businessman. Not since that time had I found another doctor who rivaled his ability and desire to heal others.

At the height of my desperation and frustration, I finally found a caregiver, a neurologist at the University of Arizona, who listened. By hearing me, he saved my life.

#

"We don't know."

I never thought I'd hear a neurologist confess he was anything but all-knowing. Those words were so important to me, after years of asking "Why?" and not getting answers.

Dr. Labiner was the first to explain that my questions were ignored because no one knew the answers. No one knew why I had seizures. The brain was still a great mystery. He told me my symptoms were not as uncommon as other doctors led me to believe, when they wanted to write me off as psychologically disturbed. The things they found so unusual about my case— adult onset, nocturnal, awareness, clusters—happened to many other people. He recommended books for me to read, rather than the drug pamphlets with paragraphs about epilepsy the other doctors passed out. He had conversations with me without making me feel like he needed to be somewhere else. He treated me like I was an adult person. I needed treatment for my epilepsy. The only things he had that would help me, unfortunately, were anticonvulsant medications.

He convinced me I needed drug therapy by promising to try everything—even new and experimental drugs—until something worked. There were some I had not tried, and some new ones coming. We would figure out which one worked best for me. I didn't have to take one that made me feel my life was worthless. It would not be easy, or fun, but we would keep trying them until we found one I could live with.

Things got worse before they got better. But when something did not work, we tried something else. If I was not going to take it, or if I was going to mess with the dosing myself, there was no point in keeping me on a drug that I could not tolerate. I felt like he wanted me to succeed and be healthy. And he understood that being happy is a big part of being healthy. We would work together until I was both.

The most brutal years of my seizures were ahead of me. The number increased, and the severity increased as I tried new medications, going on them, coming off them. Some of them had invisible side effects I couldn't see myself.

#

One warm Saturday evening at the club where everyone I knew hung out, I ran into Fonda, a friend I made while working at my dad's office. We sat at a small table away from our friends and the pounding dance music to catch up by having an actual conversation while she waited for a ride to a party. I jumped when a slimy package of meat dropped onto the table.

"Think she'll like it?"

I looked up at the man standing over us. Dressed in black, he had long blond hair and light blue eyes that were hard to look away from.

He smiled. "Hello."

My friend made a quick introduction. "This is Katie Taylor. Jeff Smith."

"It's a beef tongue."

Their friend was celebrating her birthday, and this was apparently Jeff's idea of a present.

"Hmmm." Fonda thought for a moment. If only gift cards existed in the 1990's, anyone could be trusted to run to the store and buy a present. Even Jeff Smith. "Not really what I had in mind."

"What do you think?" Jeff asked me.

I very rarely found myself at a loss for words. I didn't know the friend who would receive this shockingly awful gift. Maybe there was a joke here I didn't get. And this strange man's blue eyes and cryptic smile threw me off my game. "I... think it's very... memorable."

Jeff looked pleased with himself and focused on Fonda. "Are you ready to go?"

Fonda and I said our goodbyes and she left with Jeff carrying the beef tongue she refused to touch. I headed back to my friends on the dance floor, hoping I would see him again.

I never guessed I would someday rely on the man I met that night to help me get through some very difficult places in my life. He would become one of the best friends I've ever had.

I quizzed Fonda about her unusual friend when I next saw her. She told me he was a photographer, and loved one woman who broke his heart and afterward vowed to never marry or even fall in love again. I told her I liked a challenge. She offered to introduce us properly and took me to visit him at work.

#

Jeff owned and operated Fotosmith, a successful photography studio. A gifted photographer with an artist's eye for color and composition, he worked incredibly hard and knew his craft backwards and forwards. He was intense while shooting film, profoundly focused and not above an occasional tantrum if things weren't going his way.

It turned out that, when I met him, Jeff needed help with customer correspondence and general office work, so I began working for him part time. Like many with creative minds, his business lacked structure in certain places. I liked the idea of getting up a little later and wearing whatever I wanted to work. I made myself fit in where he needed assistance. I occasionally helped him with photo shoots, but I primarily handled his billing and mail.

I learned things from Jeff. I learned how to frame an image, and how to be cognizant of all light sources. I learned how to have an eye for details, to see a misplaced hair or a random leaf on the ground behind a model. I learned the hardest words to accept from another person: "I love you, but I'm not in love with you." And I learned how much I needed people who loved me, and how unprepared I was for anyone in love with me.

Chapter 17—Facing Death

On December 11, 1993, I got a call from my mom. One of the men my father was playing golf with in Phoenix called to tell her my dad passed out on the golf course and had been taken to the hospital.

I wanted my mom to wait until we heard from the hospital so we knew what happened before we got on the road. She refused. She would pick me up in fifteen minutes so I could ride to Phoenix with her because she didn't want to drive alone. Something, she could tell, was very wrong.

Something was very, very wrong.

My father had a massive heart attack. He was undergoing heart surgery by the time we reached the hospital. He had turned fifty-six less than a week before. I have never felt anything like the fear I experienced that day. Everything I knew to be true in my life went white, and empty.

#

I noticed my hand was shaking when I reached into the glove compartment for the registration I knew I'd find there. He was always so particular about things like that. When I saw the look on the cop's face, I thought about how I must look for the first time that day. Un-showered, no make-up, sleep deprived, wearing my brother's t-shirt and jeans I'd had on for at least two straight days, and underwear I bought that morning at Walgreens when I went to get myself a toothbrush. (Had that been today?)

"Who is Jacob Taylor?" the cop was asking.

"My father... he had... he had a heart attack." I hadn't ever said that before and my voice caught in a funny way. I wondered why I was telling this stranger who didn't even care. Would he think I was lying to get out of a ticket? "I really didn't know how fast I was going. It's just that..." I exploded into fierce tears, reaching toward hyperventilation. The speed limit meant nothing. What I looked like meant nothing.

When the cop told me to get out of the car, he was going to call someone to pick me up because he thought I was too hysterical to drive, I became more hysterical. Not because I was in the barren stretch of nothing between Phoenix and Tucson, but because I had to drive my dad's car back. I was the only one who could drive a stick shift.

"You can't, because there's no one to call." Tears continued streaming down my face.

Another officer came and waited with us. When I finished crying, he gave me the ticket and let me go. I promised to go the speed limit and to be careful. It was the holidays, after all.

#

Life finds funny ways to teach us perspective. I needed to be well. It was my father's turn to be taken care of, and I had to show everyone that I had my life together and convince them I felt great. It was easy to do because it was what everyone needed to hear.

My father came home. What could have been the worst Christmas of my life was instead filled with gratitude.

My mother managed to pull off all the usual magic while caring for my very ill father.

Jeff surprised me by accepting my invitation to be my plus-one for Christmas Eve dinner at my mother's beautiful table. As always, a delectable collection of deliciousness surrounded by bright, carefully chosen decorations lay spread before all my siblings, parents, and grandmother. Meeting my family this way seemed like a very boyfriend thing to do, and I knew Jeff never intended to fill that role in my life.

My grandmother was in rare form that night. She found a new way to grab everyone's attention with an unexpected announcement in her soft southern drawl.

"I took a bath today, and when I got out I was rubbing lotion all over myself, and it felt sooooo good, I've decided I'm a lesbian."

I laughed so hard I fell back in my chair. Jeff chuckled and replied, "I'm a lesbian too."

No one else smiled, especially my mother. She wanted us all to stay calm and quiet for my father, who was there despite his surgery.

Later, when my mother told my grandmother what a lesbian was, my grandmother told her she had a dirty mind and didn't know what she was talking about. A good Christian Southern woman would never do anything like that. She obviously heard the line somewhere else and saved it for a shocking moment, without having any idea what she was saying.

Jeff spent a good part of the evening in private conversation with my grandmother, which was fine with all of us. They became fast friends after that evening. I never expected her to be the first person in my family to accept a long-haired artist as my 'date.'

#

Dr. Labiner came across a diet he thought might help me. My inability to tolerate drugs frustrated both of us. I'd never had a doctor who suggested anything else, but the Ketogenic Diet showed great promise in some patients with epilepsy.

I already knew food had enormous effects on my seizures. Certain things, like hot dogs, always meant seizures the next night. MSG had an instant effect, making me feel as though I walked through a tunnel and muting all the sounds around me. Could food be the answer?

Unfortunately, the Keto diet didn't decrease my seizures. Regardless, I was grateful my doctor had an open mind when it came to treatment. I never thought I'd find a neurologist who suggested anything other than drugs, and more drugs.

Back to the drawing board. Again.

#

My parents still paid most of my rent in 1994, even when I didn't work for my father. I wrote poetry and short stories and screenplays and lived in my head. My seizures became routine, and my sleep sporadic. I still had several seizures a week, often several in one night. They did decrease when my doctor added Phenobarbital to the Tegretol I had once again switched to, making me even more tired, but somehow more able to focus.

I still maintained a somewhat "healthy" social life. I did drink more alcohol than I should, considering my medications. But I usually ate responsibly, except for the nights we all scraped change together to grab cheap tacos.

My closest friend lived in my apartment complex. I never imagined a single mom could find so much time to care for others. But Kelly amazed me in many ways.

She encouraged me to write. I didn't have many people in my life pushing me in that direction. She convinced me I could write prose as well as dialogue, and I started moving away from screenplays toward short stories. I even started a book, which I swore I would never do.

I adored her son, Sam, who was the same age as my sister's son, Scott. It was fulfilling to have a child in my life so close by. I relished every moment I spent with my nephew, but he lived an hour away. Sam lived downstairs. He and Kelly helped me realize I could be a mom someday and do just fine.

Chapter 18—Reunion

Life was working out. My meds did not make me seizure-free, but they did decrease the frequency. I only had as many seizures in a month as I'd had in a week, or sometimes a night. I could function, and the depression subsided considerably. I began writing more than a journal again, and I began to maintain my own freelance PR clients and pick up copywriting and copyediting jobs I could work on from home. I could decide my own hours and do far less driving.

I still faced difficulties with the doctors within my HMO. My physician did not return calls. I filled my medications through his office so I could pay the insurance copays, since my neurologist, Dr. Labiner, was out of network. My physician would fail to send refills after I called, and would fail to note when my medications changed. I would wait for the pharmacy to reach him, then not get my medications because he had something else written on my chart. When I told him my neurologist suggested I get another MRI, he told me the new MRI machine at the hospital was really impressive, but he could not give me a referral because the test was too expensive. I did not cry any tears when he retired.

I was back to finding a new general practitioner, and within the network where my former neurologists remained prominent providers, I was considered toxic and non-compliant, even by general physicians.

I showed the letter I received from the neurologist saying I was mentally unstable to the first physician I tried to see, and a letter showing I had been diagnosed with epilepsy, to make sure he knew I actually had a disease, not just a need for attention, which my former doctors in his network never fully turned loose. He read the letter and laughed. He thought I needed a better sense of humor. Later, I received this letter from him:

97

M.D.

May 18, 1994

Miss Katie Taylor
331 S. Alvernon #3
Tucson, Arizona 85711

Dear Miss Taylor:

After considering our conversation of yesterday, more completely
I have concluded that for personal reasons I cannot be your
physician. I will be available to you, should there be a need,
until you can make any arrangements, and suggest that you consult
with Partners to find another primary physician as soon as
possible.

Sincerely,

M. D.

/en
cc Partners Health Plan of AZ
   5210 E. Williams Cir.Ste.300
   Tucson, Arizona 85711

I decided not to show the letters to anyone else. I finally
found a new doctor, after a few who were on the HMO list of
available general practitioners declined me, claiming their
practices were full.

#

My ability to forget people became more absolute. When
my ten-year high school reunion came around in the summer of
1994, my best friend since seventh grade, Michelle, wanted me
to go. She thought I would remember more people than I told
her I would, once I met them again.

People did not understand when I said I couldn't remember them, or remember something we experienced together. There were so many conversations consisting of another person asking me, "You don't remember? What about this? What about that? How about him or her? REALLY?" I know it did not make sense to most people when I told them I did not remember an entire ski trip, or a senior trip. Especially when I did not remember going at all, or even remember visiting the places I went. People thought maybe I just didn't remember one part, or place or person. People wanted to prod me until I relented and a light came into my eyes as I said, "Oh, yeah! I remember that part! That was so amazingly fun!" I stopped telling people I did not know them or have context for them to live in in my mind to avoid this constant barrage.

Instead, I smiled and nodded, and faked my way through. I expended an enormous amount of mental energy, playing off others, allowing them to tell my part and theirs.

A room full of potential embarrassment at a reunion did not have any appeal to me. I tried to convince Michelle that, although she was coming from out of town and I wanted to spend time with her, the weekend would be a nightmare for me. She persisted, until I finally bought a ticket.

In high school, I knew everyone. I had a position on student council, I was president of The Thespian Society, I was a song leader, and I had been in that school system since first grade. By the time our reunion came, I only remembered about five people out of my class of two-hundred-seventy-five.

One of the few people I remembered the summer of our reunion was the boy who pulled out the chair of the girl who had a seizure in second grade. I decided I could go just to find him, and ask him about the little girl who falls down over and over in my mind. I thought he would be able to tell me her name and to fill in the holes in the story.

I knew he would be there from the list of attendees. I searched nametags as inconspicuously as possible, trying not to make eye contact with anyone. I didn't wear my own nametag and kept my head down as much as possible. I rushed up to him when I saw him and burst into my story. Did he remember?

He did not. He said it sounded like something he would do. I could see his recklessness as a kid was something he would like to forget. He asked me if I remembered the girl standing next to him who was now his wife and of course I did not, but I said yes and shook her hand. He let me know his older sister, who was apparently my older sister's best friend growing up, was fine, and I told him my sister was fine, too.

I found Michelle on the dance floor with her fiancé Jeff and hugged her goodbye, promising to meet them for breakfast, and then walked too fast to be recognized to the exit. I spent less than thirty minutes total at the event, and that had been too much.

I left wondering how the girl in the yellow sweatsuit became so important to me. Did it really happen, or did my subconscious mind create her story to make me feel less alone? Why couldn't the boy from my memory, one of the few people from my past who had any place in my mind, any backstory, remember her like I did?

I went to bed that night more lonely than I knew was possible.

#

The air hung heavy with the promise of rain. The sun would be falling beneath the distant thundercloud in about twenty minutes, becoming a fiery mass shooting over the exposed mountains to the west. I sat on my porch breathing in the solitude that comes from humidity laden with the heady smell of wet creosote bushes. Rain would come.

The phone rang.

"Are you ready?"

Was I? "Yeah."

"Meet me at the studio."

Jeff finished loading his gear as I arrived. "Let's go."

I kept telling myself I should be scared. But Jeff rarely took anyone with him to chase lightning. I couldn't say no.

We drove in silence toward the thunderhead. A few drops of rain fell on the windshield of Jeff's truck, not enough to turn on the wipers. He focused on the storm ahead, reading the clouds.

The sun went down kicking and screaming bright orange across the underbelly of the storm. Off to the east an electrical charge flashed in the clouds. "Did you see that?" Jeff asked.

"Yeah."

He pulled over on the side of the road and dragged his equipment out of the camper on the back. Film was already loaded and ready to go. I pretended to know how to help, trying my best to remember the names of the items he asked me to find.

After the sun set, the charge swimming in the clouds escaped and lightning struck in the distance. A spidery web grabbed for the ground. Inevitable thunder followed.

I felt a kinship to the clouds, gray and stiff like the folds of my brain. Electricity crashed into them and they spit it back out, shaking the ground with thundering protests.

Jeff seemed at home. The stress I saw during studio and location shoots had no place here. I had never felt so at ease with him. Perhaps his love for storms made him more able to understand me and what I lived with.

Desert monsoons are humbling. The greatness of the moment, the fleeting passage of time, the knowledge no two moments are ever the same, creates a secret society among desert dwellers. Jeff and I quietly became better friends that night.

#

That fall my first niece was born, healthy and screaming as all babies should. I remember waiting in the hospital, sitting with my nephew in his pajamas, and my brother-in-law coming out and telling us her name. Scott jumped up and down on the chair next to me, laughing and saying "Hooray! Hooray!" over and over again.

She would be Hannah Scarlett, like my mom, and like me. My heart sang.

ACT IV:

FROG SONG

To live without hope is to cease to live.

~ Fyodor Dostoevsky, novelist and epileptic

Chapter 19—Rain Dance

Clouds built up to the south, bringing another monsoon from Mexico. The clouds reminded me of Texas for some reason. Kelly agreed.

Kelly and I sat on the concrete steps behind her and Sam's apartment. She lived in Texas in her late teens. Her memories were of boys and popularity contests, unlike the slideshow I carried of happy childhood moments. We talked about what a difference a few years made in how we perceived the world. As always, I felt calm in her presence. Her voice and movements flowed like a stream over a deep pool of water, and her patience with Sam was infinite.

Most of our neighbors were retired. The others were ancient relics. There was no pool, or clubhouse, or weekly mixers. There was quiet, and Kelly and I relished it.

She was the only mom I knew who was my age, and the only single mom I'd ever known at all. She was finishing school, with Sam at her side. She seemed to find extra hours in every day. Wrapping myself in self-pity over my seizures seemed frivolous when I spent time with them.

The wind stirred. I pushed myself up and strode toward the center of the large grassy area between the apartments. "C'mon, Sam, let's do a rain dance."

"What's that?" he asked, hands on his hips, trying to decide if I was joking. Sam was a serious child, wise far beyond his years, and he didn't always appreciate my humor.

"It's a magic dance that makes the clouds notice they haven't dropped any rain yet. When they see us, if they are holding any drops, they'll let them go." The leaves of the giant eucalyptus trees surrounding us shivered.

I started stomping around in circles and singing a wordless song. Sam wasn't really buying it, but my dance looked like silly fun. He joined me. I was thrilled when he began to laugh. So were the clouds. Raindrops began to fall, one at a time, hard and heavy. We continued to laugh and do our dance, and Kelly didn't stop us, even when we were drenched.

#

That fall, my grandmother's health began to fail, and she went into the hospital. Long hours were spent in waiting rooms while batteries of tests were performed. I think the official diagnosis was "body wearing out."

Although I adored her, I know no one ever considered my grandmother an easy person to deal with. Aging did not soften her, and she fiercely fought against getting old. To spite her declining health, she dressed to impress, fixed her hair and makeup in the morning, and wore high heels every day, even when she knew she would be riding in a wheelchair.

My grandmother now needed full-time care. My parents moved her into a room in their house, and my mom catered to her night and day.

My mother exhibited enormous patience with this formidable, demanding matriarch who ran the world as if she were the sun, and the rest of us tiny planets. But the oppression she tolerated from her mother began to sink her into depression, and I could see her unraveling, and my parents' relationship suffering. There was no other way in my mom's mind—she had to take care of her mother.

While helping my grandmother turn in bed, my mother slipped two disks in her neck. For the first time, my mom needed to be on the receiving end of constant care. My youngest brother was in school, my other brother was working, and my sister had a family of her own. The duty fell to me to care for both of them. I had to move back in with my parents.

My best friend Michelle's mother, Beverly, was a masseuse, and she offered to work on my mom, who could barely stand to be touched. Every day for weeks, she would massage my mom for as long as she could take the pain.

Michelle's mother defied description. She was blonde and curvy, with green eyes as piercing as my mother's. She believed in mermaids before they were cool, and, although she lived in the desert for much of her life, she belonged to the ocean. She also saw inside people in a way that made them believe they had a soul.

She actually managed to coax the discs in my mom's neck back into place through massage. Beverly proved to be a lifesaver for my mom.

#

I worked part time at a job Jeff found for me. It was hard to stay awake, or to concentrate. I arrived three mornings a week and secretly watched my coworkers do their jobs before I could understand what I was supposed to do. An enormous amount of mental energy went into pretending to know what they expected me to accomplish, remembering my coworkers' names from week to week, and knowing which person was my boss. I never moved past the lost feeling of the first day at a new job.

I proofread textbooks. It was mind numbing, which made me more anxious to sleep. But the task was simple and seemed like a job for a smart person. I once was that kind of person.

I did not have to talk. As much as I liked to hear the sound of my own voice, my tongue swelled from biting it during my seizures, and I sounded drunk all the time. Pretending to be hyper-focused on the reading kept me from making any work friends. I felt separate, lonelier with these people than I felt at home by myself. But a small paycheck with my name on it waited for me at the end of the month.

Of course the job could not last. I don't remember much of anything, except that it ended in a tearful breakdown, sobbing in front of everyone and telling them I couldn't do it anymore. I was barely there for a month, maybe two.

#

Two days before Christmas in 1995, my grandmother died. The joy of the season came to a screeching halt. Trying to balance the loss of a major force in our lives with my young nephew's and niece's excitement over Santa's visit took some major acting skills for all of us.

My grandmother wasn't the kind of person who would want us to feel joyful she had passed into a better place. She would have expected us all to mourn dramatically. Even though my mother and I felt her loss more than anyone else in the family, her lingering presence still intimidated everyone enough to dial our smiles and joyfulness down to an absolute minimum.

The New Year would certainly be different without her. My mother was set adrift into a world without a gravitational pull. She held on to us even tighter.

An upstairs, two-bedroom apartment opened up at my beloved apartment complex. I found a roommate and moved into the larger unit, happy to be near Kelly and Sam again.

I continued to write and to pick up freelance jobs. Kelly taught me how to go about becoming a substitute teacher. I loved the flexibility, and the lack of commitment. I continued my search for an anchor to steady me.

Chapter 20—Faith

As a child, my family attended church faithfully. Sunday services, altar guild, bible study, and volunteer work took us to church more than once and sometimes four times a week. Belief in the Christian God was expected, never discussed, and never questioned.

The rote routine comforted me through the first years of my seizures. So many things could not take hold in my brain, but the recitation of the service will forever stand rooted in my mind.

I often attended an evening service alone. I could wear what I wanted, sit by myself, and pray for my life back. I could beg to understand why my brain broke, and beg to have the seizures stop. Meditation, and the comfort of something I remembered, gave me hope.

One evening, shortly after my grandmother left this world, I sat alone on the smooth wooden pew, going through the regular prayers. The service reached a forgettable moment. As a congregation, we mindlessly chanted, "...I confess that I have sinned against you, in thought, word, and deed..." I stopped. I felt like I woke up from a long, accidental nap. *Bullshit!* I thought. *I haven't done one thing this week that any decent god would expect me to apologize for!* I thought about all the times I had recited that prayer, even as a small child... all the times I had humbly confessed sinning, without ever stopping to think what I was saying.

I walked out.

My mother could not understand why I turned my back on my faith. Church and God existed as one in her eyes, inseparable. She wondered, aloud, how I ever expected to be well without God's help. I insisted he would help me even if I didn't go to church. If I was wrong, she would just have to pray even harder for me.

Chapter 21—Summer 1996

Summer won't quit. Every year, by August, when the rains have gone, everyone begins to question why they live here in this desert heat. Days drag their feet, shuffling slowly from sunrise to sunset.

I have memorized every square inch of my ceiling. It looks like it is simply painted white, but there are pallet marks in the plaster, so subtle, only there for someone who lies in bed, staring up for hours. There is a smear shaped like a shark over my bed, and one shaped like a dog. Sleep is not my friend today. At 4:39 a.m., the sun is on its way up.

Outside my open window I hear barking. Big dog, I think, until the clap of a bigger dog joins in. Not an answer, a reinforcement. I wait for the next sound; it is more like the screams of frightened children than the barking dogs now pitched to frenzy. Cold deceivers, coarse fur thrown loosely over wire bodies. I wonder now how long my eyes have been open, watching each window glow evenly with the threat of morning. The barking is tired, the howls reduced to victorious laughter. A car passes, halts, continues, each brief stop marked by a firecracker snap as newspapers slap sleepy porches. The dogs are quiet. Mourning doves question and answer themselves like only children at play. "You sure? Yes, yes, yes." The curtain moves aside as the cat deserts his post on the windowsill, unruffled by the previous canine chorus, his mews soft and consistent, wanting to go outside while everything is still cool. "Can I? Huh? Can I?" Like the changing guard I replace him, resting my chin on painted wood, stretching my body across the still-made bed pushed against the wall so I won't fall out again. One thin dark scrap of cloud clings to the south, a rip in the fabric of the otherwise naked sky. The horizon glows like a distant forest fire. The stillness is complete. Until the prisoner enters, moving without defense over the sandy gravel, hanging his head with false humility, hiding the tired craving in his eyes. You won't sing your serenade at my window, Song Dog. Your cruel voice requires accompaniment. Alone you are shackled by vulnerability. Find your hiding place from light. Your trickery is useless now without shadows of darkness and the strategic maneuvers of your scrappy army. You feel my stare like warm fingers, running over the sunken hollow of your hunger. Like a gray cloud shadow you are gone before I can count the washboard ridges of your ribs, pursued only by your footprints. I watch the thinning south cloud turn circus-candy pink over the whitening horizon—the only color the sky will show this day— before rolling back to my pillow searching for my misplaced sleep. I still have two hours before I need to get up and work. My freelance projects couldn't be put off any longer, or my clients would be unhappy.

#

When I ignored my phone, Jeff showed up at my door. He woke me with his knocking. I crawled out of my dark, quiet closet when I realized he obviously didn't intend to leave.

"Hi."

"Hi." I tried to sound awake.

"What's up?"

"Nothing." Short answers are important when trying not to slur your words.

"Hmm."

We took in my appearance at the same time. I couldn't remember the last time I changed my clothes, or showered.

"Let's go for a walk."

"No thanks."

"C'mon. Get your shoes."

"No."

"You need to get outside."

I knew he was right. But fresh air might hurt. I felt so safe inside. And I was so tired. Walking sounded hard. And stairs stood in the way to the ground.

"Let's go." He wasn't taking no for an answer.

"Fine." I splashed water on my face in the bathroom and quickly brushed my teeth, then balanced against the couch to slip into flip flops. "Let's go."

When we walked outside, the light blinded me for a moment, and I grabbed the stair railing for support. Walking wasn't as hard as I imagined, and fresh air felt amazing. I couldn't remember why I had been avoiding the outdoors.

"New meds, huh?" Jeff asked.

Could that be it? Was that when this started? I couldn't remember. It seemed like I had been taking them forever. "Maybe." My mind felt too exhausted to contemplate something that complicated.

"Are they working?"

"No. Maybe. I don't know."

When we returned to my apartment I realized how still and stale the air was. I smelled ripe, too. Jeff hugged me anyway. "Let's go to a movie. I'll pick you up at 7:00."

"Okay."

"Want me to stay while you take a shower?" It was a thoughtful, but embarrassing offer.

"No. I'm capable of dressing myself." Wow. I managed a full sentence.

When Jeff left, I realized if I died right then, he would be the one to find my body, when he came back to pick me up for the movie. I would be okay with that.

Those days, I often thought about who would find me if I decided to die. The irrational fear that it would be Kelly and her son Sam, or my sister and her children, kept me alive. I couldn't ruin their lives by taking mine. I sometimes curled up in bed

113

sobbing at the thought of my niece and nephew attending my funeral. I stayed in the world for them.

I started wondering about my motives. Were suicidal thoughts a side effect my doctor talked to me about? I couldn't remember.

Maybe it was the meds. Which meant I'd have to start over again.

Shit.

Chapter 22—Control

My HMO agreed to allow me to participate in another trial for a new drug. This wasn't my first attempt at finding the new wondrous answer to drug therapy. But it was my last.

Lamictal does not work for everyone. But it actually works for me. With the proper dosage finally in place, I got my seizures down to about ten a month, rather than four a night. Dr. Labiner did not consider them controlled, but I did. And I never, as far back as I could remember, felt better in my life.

When Dr. Labiner first asked me to talk to his medical students, I wasn't sure what to expect, but I was excited to tell my story.

The interest and surprise on the students' faces was enough to make me understand that I was not a file. I was a person. They asked meaningful questions. Their horror at the letter I shared with them, from the doctor asking my physician for a brain tumor patient, gave me hope for the future.

I learned that day, facing those students who would someday have patients of their own, I am not seizures. They don't define me because I am more than a diagnosis. I am not a woman with a need for attention, but a person with epilepsy.

My ultimate goal was for students to walk away understanding that, until the connection between women and mental illness disappears, doctors cannot successfully treat female patients. If care-givers accepted that ovaries did not improve imagination, or cause irrational behavior, misdiagnosis could be a thing of the past.

#

For Christmas 1996, the year after my grandmother died, I gave my mother a special gift. I saw the work of a young artist I loved, Maya Franklin, and decided to give my mother a piece of her work. I made an appointment to meet with Maya at Jeff's photography studio, and went carefully through her colorful pastel drawings until I found a piece I could afford, that I thought my mother would appreciate—an angel.

My mother and I still often sparred about my decision to abandon church. Especially at Christmas, when everything I loved about practiced religion came alive. I wanted her to understand why I felt I could go with her on Christmas Eve when I wouldn't go every Sunday. I wanted her to know I still had faith in God, and still believed my grandmother, grandfather, and all the others lost to this world would always be present as angels.

Christmas allowed me to be on even ground with everyone. I didn't feel like the sick one, or the unmarried one. We were all in it together, with the stress and the silent resentment and the suppressed anger we were all so good at, precariously balanced by the true joy of nieces and nephews and siblings united against the craziness of parents.

I spent extra time with my mom that year, doing things the way they'd always been done. I helped her make my grandmother's Angel's Delight, and my great-grandmother's pralines. We made it through without my seizures mattering to anyone.

Kelly, who often called me by my middle name, gave me a journal for Christmas. In it she wrote:

Dear Scarlett,

Be great in your deeds and noble in your actions. Write with heart and conviction. Be true to yourself and your pen. I believe in you.

Angels abounded.

Chapter 23—Rainbows

Standing in my apartment, I feel the blanket of electricity that comes with my seizures begin to slowly cover me. There is a pulsating ringing in my ears, and I'm trying to scream, but no sound will come. I can hear my youngest brother, Dan, sounding as if he's far in the distance, screaming expletives, as if he's never seen me have a seizure. I can't remember why he's there. I want to scream, "Why?" I try to fight, telling my brain this is not part of my deal. I have learned to accept the nighttime seizures. But I won't do daytime seizures. Not now, not ever. I give in and go down, hurting myself somewhere, against something. Then dark silence.

I realized even in that instant of confusion at the start of my seizure how a daytime episode not brought on by drug withdrawal or an ocean of tequila changed the game my brain played with my body. I was now a danger to myself and to others. I was vulnerable to the actions of strangers. People I had never met could observe my helplessness, be witness to my mental weakness.

I knew these things, but I couldn't care. As I sank into my silent scream and darkness smothered me, I knew I would wake up in the hospital.

#

"Honey, can you hear me?" My mother's voice was as calm as always, but more insistent. She was direct and didn't give any slack, for the patient or the doctors. "Come on, Sweetheart, I know you're tired, but try to talk to me."

I'm fine." I tried to get up, but they fought me. I fought harder. "Stop it! Let me up!"

My side hurt, a bruise already crawling across my ribs. Breathing deeply hurt.

"Just relax, Baby." My dad's voice added an unexpected level of emotion to my frustration, changing my determination to despair. He'd left work to be there. This was more serious than I realized.

I started to cry.

"Hold tight until the doctor gets back. Just another minute." My mother's voice left no room for dispute, and I pushed back into the crispy white sheets. My head rested against a lumpy excuse for a pillow, and I waited. And waited.

Because electricity mauled my brain, I'm not able to consider what a daytime seizure changes. I would remember eventually the panicked thoughts coursing through my consciousness at the seizure's onset.

A doctor entered with a clipboard, my clipboard. He did not bother to look at me. The words on the papers in his hands held more value to him. "Katie, it looks like you had a seizure. What medic…" His questions faded for me, and I heard my parents racing to answer. "Let's see if Katie can answer some questions. Do you think you can answer a few things?" I nodded. "What day is it?"

"Tuesday."

"Can you tell me who these people are?"

"Mom, Dad."

"Good. You've been given an injection of Diazepam, and that will make you feel very sleepy, and probably hung over for a day or two. Get some rest, and make an appointment to see your neurologist right away. Can one of you stay with her tonight?" They answered "yes" in unison, and I was overwhelmed. *Why do they love me so much?* I couldn't stop the tears. The doctor leaned over me, staring at me with rote indifference.

"Diazepam can make you feel very emotional."

"I've taken it. It sucks."

The doctor sighed. "Rest for now and—"

"—I have nighttime seizures."

"What?"

"My seizures happen when I'm sleeping."

"I explained all that earlier when we came in," My mom added, hotly.

The doctor looked again at my chart, then sighed again. He looked exhausted. "Well, the instructions are the same. Go home, and get into bed and if you have another episode, come back. Make sure you make an appointment with your doctor. I'll have some papers for you to sign and then you can go."

"What about her side?"

"Does it hurt when you breathe?"

"Everything hurts, but I can't feel it yet." When you've had a seizure, you make profound use of senselessness.

He sighed. "Ibuprofen should work fine. You probably bruised a rib. Call your doctor if you think you need something stronger."

And he left.

My parents shook their heads. They knew the truth glaring down at me. I still couldn't think that far ahead. At that moment I did not really care.

The Diazepam kept me from caring about anything other than sleep. My mom tried to keep me awake in the car, so I didn't fall asleep and have another seizure, until my father reminded her I was in their car at that moment because I had a seizure while I was awake.

I slipped under the chemical blanket wrapped around me. This would all wait until a better day. *Hopefully,* I thought, *that day will be tomorrow.* Somewhere, my ribs were hurting, and I tried to think about shifting so they got relief.

My first daytime seizure, when Kim came to visit and we had too much fun at happy hour, was easily written off as a lack of medication combined with an overabundance of tequila. This daytime seizure came out of nowhere. We were all sad and baffled. Could this be the road ahead? No one could say. For now, I had to follow the rules I always considered made for other people. No driving, more medication, no high places or swimming pools. No baths without supervision. I felt suddenly infantile and useless. I hated my brain.

From the journal Kelly gave me:

January, 1997.

The other day (day before the day before yesterday) I had a waking seizure in public. I went to sit outside to wait for my dad for a ride to Dr. Chang's because I can't drive now, and I wanted to feel really sorry for myself, how could this happen and all that. And I looked up, and there was this beautiful rainbow, from nowhere! And I got mad at God, because how can he do this, show me a rainbow on a cloudy day, one that no one else could see. I asked Nick, the kid across the way, and loaned him my sunglasses, but he couldn't see it. That's something that made me say, "Thank you," even though I wasn't feeling very thankful. I must learn to be gracious without being weak. I must learn to notice more rainbows, even if I have to search.

\#

Everything changed that day. I changed. I felt a sense of surrender, a need to see something positive in everything, everywhere, to keep myself here.

My memory, at that point, consisted of whatever happened on the day at hand and sometimes the day before. I could keep things like friends and family, and my neighbors and pets all in places in my mental space, but most of my mind felt like an abandoned building, a broom against the wall, dust growing thick on the handle and bristles.

Switching medications, going on and off medications, increasing medications, decreasing medications, blood level tests, kidney and liver function tests, all seemed pointless after my waking seizure. I'd found Lamictal the summer before and felt like a version of myself, but now the drug obviously was not working. I turned to Eastern Medicine.

Acupuncture did not cure my seizures, but I began to understand the way energy flows through the body. I could visualize true meditation. Not just sitting quietly, but feeling the balance or imbalance of power inside me. I have taken that with me through life.

No matter what time of day I went for treatment, I fell into a deep sleep with the needles perfectly placed along my meridians. I had a seizure during a session and woke up with a gasp, as if coming up out of water. My seizure immediately stopped. I looked up at the doctor as he pressed where my nose met my upper lip, where the top of a mustache would be. I felt aware and clear-minded. I learned there is a pressure point there, and I have been able to use it throughout my life to wake myself up if I think I will have a seizure.

#

In February 1997, my sister's youngest son was born, healthy and screaming as all babies should. Cole added volumes to the joy of our family. I had even more to be grateful for.

Michelle married in 1997. I traveled up to Phoenix to be a bridesmaid in her wedding, wearing a dress almost the same soft pink as my prom dress. She was, of course, a stunning bride.

The days before the wedding provided a plethora of anxiety for me. I imagined dozens of people who knew me who I did not remember, and I dreaded being the completely single friend without even my standard wedding date, my handsome friend Bart, as my plus-one. I would have to work harder than usual at pretending to be someone I no longer knew anything about...

121

me. With a little too much help from the open bar, I found no one cared who I used to be, and I had a great time.

I never shared a hotel room with anyone because of my seizures. I was alone when I woke up the next morning with my back completely frozen in a muscle spasm, unable to stand or move. I managed to call someone, and Michelle's mom Beverly had the hotel staff let her into my room.

Beverly brought a homeopathic doctor with her, who asked me what I can now only remember as being very unusual but relevant questions. I felt calmer after talking to him, but when your back spasms, only time can heal. They had to call someone to pick me up in Phoenix and take me back to Tucson. The person I always called, who always came, was my mom. I felt like such a hypocrite. I spent hordes of time and energy trying to convince everyone I could manage my life myself, but when I needed someone, she always got the first call. She was immediately on her way.

The doctor left Beverly and me waiting alone together in my hotel room. She stood next to the bed where I still lied frozen and looked at me for a long moment.

She spoke gently. "You have to let your mother find her own angels."

I returned her gaze for as long as I could bear to, silent, dumbfounded, and then I burst into tears. She had looked inside me, and said the most profound words I could have imagined.

I had known her since I was twelve, and we were far from strangers. Of course she knew and loved my mother, too. But this was about me and my pain. She could see the source of my anguish more clearly than I could, and she put my inner struggle into a single sentence.

That remains one of the most memorable things anyone ever said to me.

My mother arrived a couple of hours later and picked me up. She took me back to her house where she could care for me. As I shuffled in her door, drugged on as much Ibuprofen as I could take and then a little more, the first thing I saw was the angel drawing I had given her for Christmas years before. Beverly's words came back to me. I needed to let my mother go. I needed to move forward without her, for myself, but for her, too. She needed to find her own life. And I needed to claim mine without blaming her.

#

I needed to center myself. The place I found that most offered me peace grew from the desert only a mile from my childhood home. When my back recovered enough to drive, I stopped there on my way home.

Despite working with Diego Rivera in Mexico in the 1960's, artist Ted DeGrazia couldn't find a gallery to represent him in Tucson where he grew up as an Italian immigrant, so he built his own on a compound at the foot of the Santa Catalina Mountains. He first built the Mission in the Sun, a chapel honoring Father Kino and dedicated to the Virgin of Guadalupe, from the desert itself, crafting the adobe bricks from the dirt of the land he considered his muse.

DeGrazia's work raised the ghosts of the indigenous peoples of our distant past, who thrived through the Sonoran Desert's inevitable months of inhospitable heat without ice or air conditioning. The childlike figures he was known for painting made those who didn't appreciate art roll their eyes and proclaim their five-year-olds could do better.

I never liked his popular artwork, the colors too pastel for my taste and the figures strangely haunting, like faceless dolls. But his gallery showed a different side of his brushes, with gripping, sophisticated paintings and sculptures.

Churches I had known all had things in common: An altar with finely embroidered cloths and silver vessels, wooden seats, and big doors. Entering the Mission in the Sun felt familiar in some ways, and foreign in others. The rosaries and tall glass candles with pictures of the Virgin Mary crowded on the altar escaped my understanding. These belonged specifically to the Catholic Church and I did not, so I couldn't explain their significance. Yet, I didn't feel like an imposter. I completely belonged there the moment I walked in.

The roof was open to the sky, and inhospitable rough wooden beams served as benches. DeGrazia's paintings, mostly children with angel's wings, covered the plaster walls. This tiny space felt more genuine to me than any sanctuary I ever entered. The chapel took what I knew from years of Sundays in a big beautiful building with smooth wooden pews and glistening silver decorations and boiled it all down into a tiny mud house with a dirt floor.

I was almost always the only person there, but that day, when I walked in, I found a young man kneeling at the wax-covered altar littered with votives and photos of people who needed desperate prayers, sobbing. He heard me walk in.

"Oh—I'm sorry—I didn't mean to interrupt—" I turned to go but he stood and muttered an unnecessary apology as he rushed out. His sorrow hung heavily in the air he left behind. As I scanned the photos and tried to imagine what or who he mourned, I realized my life was good. Only one little thing needed to find its place.

I sat for as long as I could, while full clouds gathered overhead. When I walked out, the humid smell of lightning filled the afternoon. Bushes bristled in the stillness as rabbits were swallowed by their crispy grayness, only their soft white tails following them.

The impatient sky grumbled like an empty stomach. The bushes were still now. Everything waited for the storm in quiet anticipation, like movie watchers staring at the growling lion who promises the imminent film. One drop fell. Another followed. I dashed to the car as the sky opened, and visibility disappeared.

I needed to get home. The arroyos would flood that afternoon, and then the water would disappear in hours. Powerful, painful, fleeting.

Chapter 24—Frog Song

There is a fascinating animal known as the Sonoran Desert Toad, or Colorado River Toad. Even for desert dwellers, a sighting is rare. They burrow most of the year, allowing us to forget about them. But on an evening after a monsoon, if you are near an arroyo after the water has rushed through and only shallow, sandy pools of rain remain, you may hear them. Loud, surprising, unabashed, and unapologetic, they belt out their chorus of frog song. You hear it and think, oh yeah... And smile to yourself. They live there, under the surface of the ground, for nearly an entire year. You forget they exist—until you hear their music, and remember who they are, and who you are. In the morning, they are gone. An entire species' chorus disappears, back into their burrows, and you forget about them again.

But they are still there, like my mind and my memories locked inside. I still cannot see them, but every once in a while, I am taken back, and the sweetest feeling of a random moment from my childhood sings to me. And I know I have truly lived a life. I had a childhood. I went to college. Then the moment disappears, and the window closes. One more small piece of my puzzle found a way back.

The desert, where I lived most of my life, and I understand each other. The subtle change of seasons and complex beauty of the plants and animals of the Sonoran Desert give me the steady comfort of familiarity. I now love sharing the fascinating plants and creatures, some that do not exist anywhere else on earth, with my son, when we visit. The desert is where I am from.

I did not understand until my thirties that, although I knew it so well, the desert was never my soul's home. I never felt complete belonging until I finally found my way to Colorado.

ACT V:

A NEW DAY

Every great dream begins with a dreamer.
Always remember, you have within you the strength,
the patience, and the passion
to reach for the stars to change the world.

~ Harriet Tubman, American hero and epileptic

Chapter 25—Bluer Skies

If you ask anyone who lives in Aspen, Colorado, how they ended up there, they will tell you they went to visit and never left. I went to visit my aunt and uncle who owned a store selling Moroccan textiles and antiques in Aspen, to help them set up a website for their business. I was not a trained website building expert, but very few people were in 1998. I knew enough to create something decent. I planned to stay for a few weeks at the most, and then stayed for over six years, long after my aunt and uncle closed their store and moved back to Tucson to be near family.

The joy and gratitude I felt with every breath of mountain air defied definition. Every day my eyes and soul drank in the pines, and I told myself I never needed to live anywhere else. My spirit soared. Hiking up Aspen Mountain, turning around to look into the valley below, I thought, *I wish everyone I know could be here right now, but at the same time, I'm so happy to be alone.* I couldn't ever accurately describe this to anyone. Just like my seizures, I can tell people about them, but I can never make them understand how they feel.

I learned from that place. The mountains taught me to be small. They taught me that no matter what happens in my life, summer will follow spring, the leaves will drop in fall, the snowflakes will drift silently in the blue light of winter—every different little snowflake—with their perfect imperfections. Like us.

Epileptics dream of places to live where they never turn a key in an ignition. I did not own a car for the first three years I lived in Aspen because I could walk anywhere I wanted to go. For the three years I did own a car, I rarely drove, other than to move to a new parking space on the street every two days to avoid tickets, or to expand my circle of exploration, to hike new trails driving distance from me and see new angles of the Rockies.

In Aspen, I found friendly people, the best food on the planet, and the most beautiful 360-degree view you could ever wake up to see. Skiing, hiking, biking, playing volleyball in the summer, the fresh mountain air, all transformed me into a much healthier person. I walked to work, supported myself, and paid my own bills. No one in Aspen knew how accomplished those normal things made me feel.

A new view out my window, a new grocery store, strangers I knew for certain were strangers and not people I should remember and recognize, released me from a personal prison filled with constant anxiety. I did not realize how much daily energy went into just trying to remember what, and who, I thought I should know until distance lifted that burden. I could be someone different in Aspen. I could be myself.

I did miss my family, especially my nephews and niece. I wanted to watch them grow up. I missed our trips to the zoo together. But I wanted them to see me be a better, healthier, happier person. I could not do that in Tucson.

Some people feel a belonging when they stand on a beach and stare out at the waves, the rhythmic sound of the tides pulling at their soul. For me, that feeling comes from air washed by pines, a sky so blue the color can't be real, and the heady thin air at a high altitude. The mountains spoke to me. I found my home.

Epilepsy forced me to reinvent myself, without knowing myself. It sounds exciting, starting with a blank canvas and becoming whoever you really want to be. But my canvas wasn't blank—it was almost entirely black. Things I should have remembered—a childhood, a college degree, family vacations— all smeared across each other until they turned to darkness, with only fragments of color discernable here and there. Memories sprinkled around, ranked with no rhyme or reason, no value, no level of importance, no timeline. In the serenity of the new birds' songs in the leafy Aspens, I only needed to live in the present.

Being released from my past healed me. I only had to meet the expectations I set for myself, and the new person I became lived and loved without ever feeling a need to apologize for who I was, or for who I was not.

#

To say my first roommate in Aspen was a character would be a significant understatement.

A petite, blonde, adorable Brit, she was the most totally independent woman I had ever met. She cleaned houses for Aspen elites, clowned at birthday parties on the weekends (she had actually graduated from clown school,) watched *Little House on the Prairie* obsessively, and soaked herself in impressive amounts of Vodka. She kept pet ferrets as part of her act. She used seven, but only had one ferret left when I moved in because she let them roam free. The other six had run away, most likely to meet the great ferret in the sky by way of a fox. Her remaining ferret hid in seemingly impossible places and waited for opportunities to hiss at me or bite my ankles. My cat Jones was terrified of the slinky rodent, which was rather funny, since he was twice his size. She had traveled extensively, and I never knew when someone she'd met along her way would show up on our doorstep planning to stay indefinitely. Things started and stayed pretty weird in that house.

When a coworker told me an apartment where he lived was available, I threw myself at it. Even though "apartment" meant "room for rent," it seemed like a good change. I learned what it meant to jump out of the frying pan and into the fire.

Aspen was a silver mining town in the 1800's, and apparently the miners loved prostitutes. Several of the historic houses that once served as brothels were now apartment buildings, each of the rooms formerly used to pleasure the working class serving as a cubby for a present-day Aspen local.

The first whorehouse I lived in sat on the outskirts of town. A large, three-story Victorian beauty, it was now filled with a different kind of degenerate, the carny-like locals who kept the town running. Dishwashers, waiters, ski-lift operators, and an occasional ski instructor were my roommates.

My introduction to the crew didn't involve a welcoming committee. I purchased essential groceries and took them into the community kitchen, expecting to stake out a place in the cabinets. There was not a scrap of other food in the kitchen. *Huh,* I thought, *I guess no one here cooks.*

I went back the next morning to make breakfast before work to find nothing but the lid to my peanut butter jar in the cabinet. Why the lid? I learned to keep all of my food in my room.

The house was surprisingly quiet. Most of the residents spent all day and night working the three jobs required to survive. I first ran into one of my neighbors a couple of days after I moved in. He greeted me warmly and invited me to come over later and meet some of our housemates. He had baked a cheesecake (he had a unit with a kitchen) and invited everyone to come and try it.

After work, as promised, I stopped by his place. I walked into a room full of men my age. The host introduced me around, and then asked, "Do you have a glass bowl?"

"Sure!" I answered, gaining the approval of the room. I went to my room happy to have so many nice guys living in my house and returned with a glass serving bowl. They all looked at me with sincere confusion.

"What's that?"

"A glass bowl. I thought you needed it for the cheesecake for some reason."

The room literally erupted in laughter. Apparently the glass bowl they needed was a kind of pipe used for smoking pot.

The next day, another neighbor knocked on my door. "Got any papers?"

"Oh, not today's."

He looked at me for a full minute, utterly confused. I pointed to the newspaper on the floor. He laughed until he cried.

You never would've guessed marijuana was illegal in Aspen. As a nonsmoker I was definitely in the minority. The fact that a person could knock on a stranger's door and ask for rolling papers said it all.

Had I known at that point what a difference cannabis would make for many epileptics, I might have been more likely to join the party and buy myself a bowl that wasn't for serving cheesecake.

#

I had only lived in Aspen a month or two when I woke up in the hospital. Two of my coworkers from the *Aspen Daily News*, the little local newspaper where I'd been working for a couple of weeks, stood next to my bed. They weren't the two I would've guessed, both men my age, neither of whom I'd had an actual conversation with. They told me I had a seizure at work.

One chuckled. "You tried to kick their asses. You definitely gave them your best."

Apparently I'd tried to fight the EMT's who picked me up in the ambulance. I lost.

I usually remembered things from my sleeping seizures. I mentally woke up in my postictal state—the time right after the convulsions end. Most people are not aware of what's happening around them during this part of their seizure, which can last seconds, or hours. For me, this is when I start to gasp loudly for breath. I can't move or speak, but I can hear my ragged breathing, and I can hear people talking around me. But I didn't remember anything that day. I went to work, and then woke up in the hospital.

I went back to work the next day, not sure what to expect. How would people who were strangers treat me? I hadn't been forced to deal with this open public part of seizures, unlike most people with epilepsy.

Surprisingly, out of fewer than twenty people, two of my coworkers had epilepsy. They were the first epileptics I had ever met and had handled the event flawlessly. They knew what to do and what not to do. No one stuck anything in my mouth; no one tried to hold me down. If anyone thought I would swallow my tongue, something impossible to do, my epileptic coworkers had educated them. I was very lucky. I could have had my teeth knocked out, or even been choked to death by well-meaning bystanders with very bad, outdated ideas about how to react.

People at the paper obviously treated me differently, as we all do when we see someone leave in an ambulance. Knowing I couldn't always control my brain or body made them cautious. I could feel them walk past ready to catch me, or to jump out of the way. I don't know which my coworkers would have done, but I understood. Instead of humiliated, I felt cared-for.

Despite the kindness shown to me at work, hard questions came instantly. Why had this happened? Would it happen again? Was this my new normal?

#

I had my next daytime seizure while volunteering at the Aspen Film Festival. There were no convulsions. It only lasted a few seconds, just long enough for me to fall to the floor as if I'd fainted. I knew I hadn't, but I passed it off as low blood sugar to avoid questions or a trip to the hospital like I took after my seizure at the newspaper.

I played the familiar elimination game again. Could it be because of this, or that? What did I do differently? What changed? I went back through everything I ate and drank, every hour I slept or skied. I realized both my Aspen daytime seizures coincided with me taking antibiotics. I eliminated them from my life, doing my best to convince myself everything would be fine.

#

The next waking seizure came when I was in the drug store and a friend and coworker from the bookstore where I also worked at that time came up behind me and startled me. I felt ringing in my ears and a shock through my body, and my mind went black for a second. But I didn't fall. She didn't notice.

The next seizure happened about a month later while I walked down the sidewalk with my roommate and coworker from my other job, teaching three-to-six-year-olds how to ski. I dropped to the ground. Again, a single second and I got up, back to normal, no confusion, no convulsions.

Nocturnal seizures began to seem like a wonderful problem to have.

#

I never had a seizure while wearing skis, or while substitute teaching, which was my third job after I left the newspaper. I could sense when one was coming. I felt dizzy, like standing at a great height and looking over an edge, and saturated with déjà vu. The feeling could last for hours or for days, with the omnipresent threat of a storm brewing in my brain. I avoided the chairlift whenever I woke up with a foggy mind. But I don't remember ever feeling fragile while skiing or bike riding down a hill or exerting myself with extreme focus. My seizures didn't mix with adrenaline.

I felt frustrated, but not desperate. Without the concern of others overpowering me, or the need to get behind the wheel, I lived without fear.

If my new normal meant never knowing when I would find myself in a heap on the ground, Aspen was the best possible place to be.

Chapter 26—Loss

The call came in the morning. Michelle's mother, Beverly, had a massive heart attack. She had been revived in the ambulance and was in the hospital on life support. She was not expected to survive.

It's hard to grasp devastating news from a distance. I started my day in shambles, but in a couple of hours my routine took over and I forgot about Beverly for a while. In the middle of the day the memory of the morning phone call slapped me in the face, and I felt entirely guilty for having forgotten, even for a couple of hours.

It was months before she passed, her family forced to let her go. Her final words to her husband had been to tell her girls she loved them, and to tell everyone else she had a great time. Unfortunately for all who knew her, the time we had was far less than we wanted.

Chapter 27—My New Normal

I visited Dr. Labiner the next time I went to Tucson. I told him about the change in my seizure pattern. He was genuinely upset.

"Damn it!" He cursed. "I hoped this would never happen."

"Me too."

"We could try changing your medication again."

"No thanks."

We tinkered with my dosage, and things got better. After a year in the mountains, I went back almost entirely to nocturnal seizures.

Almost.

#

A couple of years after I moved to Aspen I visited my brother Andy in L.A. for a weekend during off-season. The first waking seizure I had there scared him, badly. He was the first in my family to see me have a nocturnal seizure, but he had never seen me have a waking seizure. I dropped to the floor, hitting my head hard against his bike's pedal. It hurt much worse than I let him know.

The episode ended in seconds, and I convinced him to simply continue our evening as planned, although my head swam with the dizzying promise of another seizure. It felt like standing on an enormous bubble, waiting for it to pop out from under me. It would hopefully wait for sleep.

The bubble did not last long, and my brain didn't wait until sleep to keep its promise. I fell on the sidewalk after dinner. We went back to my brother's apartment after that, cutting the evening short. That sucked. I almost never saw or talked to him, and I spent the whole time there hurting myself for the first time in a long while, then waiting for another seizure to come.

I convinced my brother not to tell my parents. I wasn't driving any more, and there was nothing they could do but worry and insist I shouldn't live alone far away in a mountain town. I knew they would want me to come home and try to find a new drug, and be close to them and to my doctor. But I didn't want that. My life now included a new kind of seizure. Nothing could change that, and I didn't want to simply find a new chemical bandage for my brain.

#

Grateful best describes the years I spent in Aspen. Every morning, waking up and walking outside, I felt unimaginable gratitude. I thanked whoever God was for the beauty of my life and this world every day. No matter who I had broken up with, or which boss had been an ass, the view out my window never disappointed me. It was so different from the desert. There was more to the world than rain or no rain. Winter, spring, summer, and fall each brought their own smells and colors and activities. I tried new things I probably never would have experienced living in Tucson. And no one told me I couldn't.

I strongly believe in uprooting when you are in poisoned soil. If I stayed in the desert, my life would have been spent trying to remember the person I once was. I needed distance to see that person could never come back.

I found a place where my soul felt full. My childhood home did not disappear. I knew I could always go back, and people there would still love me. But I had to learn to love myself as someone new before I could truly love others. That new me lived in Aspen.

While I lived in Aspen, my mother found her angel—a paintbrush. She always had the eye of an artist. She could look at a dress and go home and make one just like it. She could decorate interiors better than trained professionals. When her nest emptied, and we all made our own lives, she took a watercolor class, then another, and in no time her artwork hung on gallery walls. She found her own version of solitude and peace, and something beautiful took flight.

Chapter 28—Soul Mates

Brian, tall, young, and handsome, showed up at my apartment with a friend I invited for Thanksgiving dinner. We rearranged my table carefully set with an ironed tablecloth and hand-printed place cards to add another chair for him. I would have been annoyed if I had not received word moments before they walked in that my brother Dan's daughter Sienna, my second beautiful niece, had just been born healthy and screaming as all babies should. Nothing could have ruined that night.

Brian felt like everyone's old friend before the pie was served. I immediately recognized his talent for conversation, never missing a beat on a joke or passing on an opportunity to gently tease my friends. He stayed after everyone else left, trading jokes with me for hours. I finally sent him home, with plans to get together for a game of Scrabble.

Scrabble was a "friends" thing for me. I rarely played with men I dated because I generally didn't choose them for their brains. Brian kicked my butt. I knew then things could get serious.

By the time we met, I lived in the best apartment in town. Brian lived down-valley in a camper I never even saw. He didn't move in; he just stayed. No serious conversation about what living together meant ever took place. No rules ever needed to be laid out. I knew I found my soul mate because nothing about us was complicated.

Brian taught me that to love is to laugh. If you cannot laugh with someone, how will you get through the hard times? He made me laugh more than anyone else on the planet, and he laughed at me, too. He took my seizures in stride, seeing them as only a fraction of my whole. He gave me the courage to be myself.

The perfection of Aspen comes with a big price tag. With median home prices at one million dollars when we lived there, Brian and I knew the cost of living in Aspen exceeded our abilities to raise a family. When we decided to get married in 2003, we chose to move to San Diego for a few reasons. The weather, the beach, and the lifestyle appealed to us. We were also closer to our family in Tucson.

Hopefully, I'll eventually get back to my Rocky Mountains, but the Pacific will do for now.

Chapter 29—Setbacks
and Leaps Forward

My medical care has not been without setbacks.

I found out just how rooted our outdated ideas about seizure response are during my pregnancy.

Being an epileptic brings serious concerns to any pregnancy. Seizure medications can cause birth defects, and with my oxygen level plunging to zero during my seizures, my fetus could suffer the damaging effects of oxygen deprivation. Pregnancy hormones can also increase seizures. Old fears took new meaning, and my epilepsy again became a focal point in my husband's and my life. Thankfully, I remained seizure-free throughout most of my pregnancy.

I did have a nocturnal tonic-clonic seizure in my fifth month. I was not in danger of falling or crashing my car, but Brian and I were terrified of the effect the seizure might have on our unborn son. I called and made an appointment with my obstetrician.

The appointment started as always, with his nurse taking my vitals and writing notes for him on my chart. During her questions, she asked me a very strange question I'd never heard from a doctor. She asked if I had a bite guard. I told her "no," not understanding what she was talking about.

My dentist asked me years before if I would like for him to make me a bite guard to protect my teeth from chipping during my seizures. I tried to imagine why the nurse at my obstetrician's office would be interested in my dental care. Before I could ask she told me the doctor would make me one. My pregnant brain was searching for a connection. My OB was going to do dental work on me? Huh. That was not a part of the service, as I understood it.

The doctor entered smiling, assuring me my baby was fine. He said the nurse told him I did not have a bite guard, so he would make me one. He grabbed a handful of tongue depressors and told me he would tape them together, and my husband could take the finished product and shove it in my mouth if I had another seizure.

I wonder what I looked like at that moment. I am sure my chin hit the floor. I seethed. My emotions at that moment were probably worse for my fetus than my seizure.

How, I wondered, could he not know the protocol? How had he never learned that when you see a person have a seizure, you should simply clear the area around them, and roll them on their side, if possible? How many women had he given this outdated, ignorant information to?

I told the doctor he should never, ever offer anyone a "bite guard," and explained the many reasons why. He told me I was wrong. I told him I had worked with the Epilepsy Foundation just to educate people not to do that. He told me we did not do a very good job, because they were still teaching it the other way.

I left his office crying angry tears made larger by pregnancy hormones. I went home and began looking for another doctor. A week later, I received a letter from the doctor I had been seeing. He wanted to inform me he could not continue to be my doctor. He refused to see me again, and told me I would have to find someone else to deliver my baby, after five months in his care.

I thoroughly agreed he could not be my doctor. He should not be anybody's doctor, if he had not learned anything new in thirty years. It horrified me to know he was a teaching physician at the naval hospital in San Diego. I hope he took the time to educate himself after I left. I certainly sent him enough materials about proper seizure first aid for his whole office staff, and for his students.

I never imagined I would get another "I will not be your doctor" letter because of my seizures. It hurt, even though I had decided I did not ever want to see him again before I even made it out of his office.

I was Kate Scarlett Recore, thirty-eight, San Diego, California, and no doctor would ever get away with bullying me again.

I searched around and found a wonderful perinatologist dedicated to handling high-risk pregnancies. Losing the other doctor was a blessing. My new doctor delivered my baby boy in 2005, beautiful and screaming as all babies should, and my life has been forever changed. I understand true joy.

My son gives me more purpose than I ever imagined existed. He has changed my life.

He changed my seizures, as well. We found out very early that Jake had an allergy to dairy. If I wanted to continue nursing him, I had to give it up.

My brother Dan practices Chinese medicine. He had told me for years that if I gave up dairy and sugar, my seizures would stop. I did not want to believe him because I lived on sugar and dairy. Cream and sugar in my coffee, cream cheese on my bagel, and milk on my cereal were just the beginning of my day. I would starve to death without sugar and dairy.

But now, my life belonged to a perfect little person who could not tolerate my diet. I completely stopped all things dairy. As my brother predicted, my seizures stopped.

A simple change in my diet created an enormous change in my life. The Eastern concept of epilepsy describes the disease as "mucous misting the mind." By eliminating dairy, the primary food that built up mucous in my body, and limiting other foods that contribute to the process, like sugar, I could live a life without seizures.

I'd tried the Ketogenic Diet years before, without success. But I knew food contributed to my seizures and eliminated various things from my diet throughout the years. If I ate hot dogs, for example, I was guaranteed to have seizures at night. I avoided nitrates, nitrites and MSG. I believed in food as healthcare; I just hadn't taken it far enough. I apparently needed to eliminate an entire food group. It was mind blowing, and life changing.

#

When we became parents, Brian and I decided to make ends meet with only one paycheck, so I could stay home with Jake until he went to Kindergarten. Brian worked a ridiculous number of hours while bills turned pink and yellow and we robbed Peter to pay Paul, but somehow we made it work.

My son Jake defies description. He is the most perfect, complicated, fascinating, beautiful person I have ever known. He gives so much more than he takes. His capacity for empathy humbles and inspires me, and makes me want to be a better person every day.

He is his father's son in so many ways. They look alike and act alike. But he has some of his mother's idiosyncrasies on the inside. I knew how much he resembled me pretty early, when he was around five.

The sidewalk in front of the grocery store we frequent has a break in the concrete every three strides. Inside the break, a row of six red tiles decorate the ground. "Don't step on the red, Mommy! It's lava!" Jake jumps over the tiles, always on the far right side. I see him mentally counting his strides, avoiding the cracks in the sidewalk.

"I have lava-proof shoes, remember? I can walk on them."

Jake growls his disapproval. But I have to walk on the red tiles. I step carefully on the middle two tiles, leaving two in front of my foot, and two behind. Two tiles are the exact size of my foot. It's too hard to resist.

#

The first day I took Jake to school, I came home and sat on our back porch with a cup of tea. I was proud of myself for not shedding too many tears leaving my baby at school, excited for

145

him to learn and grow and have new friends. I took a deep breath and cleared my mind.

"What now?" I whispered.

"It's time to help other women," the universe answered. "You need to share your story."

The demand was as clear as a bell. I didn't have to search my soul or wallow in the paralyzing indecision that often plagued me through life. I had been commanded to stop protecting my story and start using it to make sure the same thing didn't happen to others just because they were female. Especially now that I had two more nieces in my life, with Andy's two girls, Lily and Presley, making the world a brighter place.

I joined Toastmasters and began writing scraps and pieces of this book when I could steal moments away from my busy life, sorting through journals and medical records and trying to make a sensible timeline of events. I set it all aside over and over, but I could not abandon the call.

I was Kate Scarlett Recore, forty-two, and I finally found my life's mission—to help other women avoid what happened to me.

Chapter 30—Being a Woman

In 1859 one quarter of all women were diagnosed with hysteria. The word itself, hysteria, comes from the Greek word for uterus, thus the term "hysterectomy." If the other medical misconceptions from the 1800's were still part of medicine today, our healthcare would be dangerous.

Today I talk about my experience with others and invite others to share with me. I have not yet known a man misdiagnosed as having psychosomatic symptoms, or an anxiety disorder, without having all other possibilities explored. However, I have met too many other women with experiences comparable to mine. One friend who has epilepsy takes her husband with her when she goes to her neurologist so she can get some information out of her visits. If she goes alone, her neurologist brushes her off within minutes. If her husband takes her, the doctor will take time to explain options and treatment to him. The doctor speaks directly to her husband, as if my friend were not sitting right in front of him. She is lucky to have a supportive husband to help her. I know I could not have found this path without the love and perseverance of my friends and family.

Illness goes far beyond the person wearing the gown, sitting on the tepid, waxy white paper stretched across the padded leather table. Illness is late-night calls to mothers and sisters, and cups of tea with friends. Strength comes from the legacy behind us, standing us on our feet when we cannot get off the floor and holding us up to fight another day.

I could not have foreseen the passion and fulfillment I would find in motherhood and in sharing my experiences. I'm grateful to the higher power that steered me toward dreams that could be answered, after my seizures transformed me into a different person I would never recognize if I traveled back in time. Or would I?

What I Want (Written in 1997)

*I don't ever want to hear the words, "You can't."
I want to find out why I can't for myself—then I'll know
I tried. I want permission to fail as an avenue toward
success, which I want to define simply. I want the
people who know me to have faith in my ability to
choose what I want for myself. I don't want to hear
what is wrong from people who don't have any idea
what is right. I want my femaleness to be a strength,
not a weakness. I want to nurture. I want to be
someone my friends and family look to for advice. I
always want to have time to listen, and to hear. I want
to be held accountable for my own happiness. I want
to expect the best from doctors and lawyers and public
officials and hairdressers. I want fairness. I want the
good news first and I want everyone around me to
understand that bad is what defines good, and life is
made of both, and they complement each other. I want
to be allowed to make life decisions based on what I
want for myself instead of what other people want for
me or from me. I want to be allowed to get angry, and
to hold a grudge when my feelings have been hurt,
because that's how I know how to prove that my
feelings are real and that they count. I want to be
allowed to expect the most everyone is capable of, and
I want everyone to expect to get as much from me as
they give to me; then I can feel good about giving even
more. I want to accept apologies when they are given
and I want to apologize only when I'm sorry. I want to
understand my spirituality better each day while
knowing I will never truly grasp its magnitude. It is
something that cannot be confined by a church or
temple. Sometimes I don't pursue what I want because*

I know it is not what someone I care about wants. Or I don't tell people about my life because I know my sadness will hurt them, and my hurt will be magnified by theirs. I want the people I care about to want everything for me. I have proven that I can handle disappointment and defeat. I don't think that should mean I no longer have time to pursue the unconventional. I want to teach whenever I can— whenever I know something someone else wants to know—because I believe patience is my greatest virtue. I think I understand justice, and I want my voice to be heard, and I want one person to say, "That makes sense." I want to leave without severing ties. I want to be connected by elastic. I want to find a way to include my epilepsy in my life, instead of fighting it. It's time to accept that my seizures are part of who I am, and they now interrupt my life only as much as I allow them to. I will not be cured by outside sources. I really believe that when they are no longer at the center of my existence—when they are simply an accepted part of my life—they will disappear. Maybe not cease—but disappear. They are my handicap only when I cannot, or am not allowed to, be responsible for how they affect my life. I have lost a lot of time and opportunity, and I am bitter, but I am no different in that respect than anyone. I want to start every day believing, I can begin from here. I want everyone around me to pursue their own dreams and set their own goals, because I want my dreams and goals and achievements to be my own. I want to be satisfied with who I am instead of with what I have. I want to celebrate small victories, and I want to help people I love celebrate theirs. I want to love, even more than I want to be loved, and I refuse to believe there is anything wrong with that. Anyone who practices happiness must accept that they will have to do what is best for themselves, because in the end that is what is best for everyone. I want to believe that if I follow my heart, the reactions from my actions will be good, because I believe my heart is good.

Things will work out. I want people to feel they know what to expect from me, but I don't want to offend or betray anyone when I do something unexpected. I want to stop caring so much about what other people think, because I am not another person, and no other person is me. I want to wake up every day and know I am someone I have invented for myself, not someone trying to do what is expected of them by someone who has their own life to lead, already, because life is a gift and I want mine for myself. Honest is not an option to me, it is a basic need, and I want friends who feel the same way. I want my own child someday, and I want him or her to be as perfect as my niece and nephews. I want to take everything my parents gave me, and I want to improve it a fraction as much as they improved what they had, if that is even possible. I want the people I care about to know I only bother getting mad at the people I care about. I want to choose the people I care about for myself. And, I want to always be able to change my mind about what I want, because that's what it means to grow and to learn, and I never want to stop doing either.

I have to tell you, self, you did a pretty good job of getting what you wanted.

Chapter 31—Owning Myself

I went to Tucson to help my parents with a very drastic downsizing. They went from their four-thousand-square-foot, five-bedroom house on two acres of land with a pool and tennis court and darkroom in a gated country-club community, where they spent decades raising children and grandchildren, to a three-bedroom apartment. The house was too much for them in every way, and we were all happy to see them move to something more manageable.

Helping go through all the things big and small collected over a lifetime hurt. My sister Nancy, who still lives in Tucson, carried most of the weight of the transition. My small contribution was more a symbolic act of solidarity than a driving force.

On a day spent trying to pry seemingly meaningless books and notions from my mother, we came to the angel painting I had given her a lifetime before. The gold-trimmed, whitewashed wooden frame and colorful matting we had so carefully picked out together was now dated. She held it and looked at it for a moment.

"Would you like to have this now?" she asked, sadly.

I looked at the piece, knowing it had no place on my walls. I spent days telling her "no" when she asked me to please take some of the things she didn't want to give away. I couldn't expect her to keep this, when she had enough of her own far more sophisticated and beautiful artwork to fill the walls of her new place.

"Sure." I took the frame from her. I knew no one else would ever see my mom, and Michelle's mom Beverly, in the strange face. I would have to make room for the angel now.

My mom looked at the angel, relieved. "I'm sorry. But I have to tell you, she always made me sad."

"Sad? Why?"

She could tell me now that I had a son of my own. "I always thought she looked like she should be holding a baby." I could see it now, the way the angel stared down at her empty cradled arms.

"Why did you keep it?"

My mom began to tear up for the thousandth time that day. "Because you gave her to me."

She had hung something she didn't like in a prominent place in her home for so long just to think of me when she looked at it. Finally, I released her. She didn't just need to find her own angels. I needed to set her free from mine. I cried, too.

#

Today, I write, and I teach. I live in the moment, choose my friends wisely, and do not feel tethered by my femaleness or family. I have even more joy in my life than I could have hoped for, and I have a loving husband and an incredible child.

I love teaching reading. I came to this when I had a friend who faked his way through college, and managed to own a successful business, with a third-grade reading level. I was shocked. He was exhausted. It takes enormous energy to maintain that kind of charade. He was the first person I helped become a better reader. He taught me the importance and power of reading follows us through life.

Now I teach kids to read. I help them struggle through, striving, learning the sounds and smoothing them out to make words, then turning those words into meaning. Learning to read is like throwing pebbles into a pond one at a time, stopping and starting, sounding and blending, until the water finally overflows its boundaries, and the words begin to pour out. Once they reach that point, words come quickly, with inflection and meaning. It is enormously gratifying.

There were times during my early struggle when I did not see the value of keeping myself here. Those moments usually came as a reaction to drugs I took sucking me into an opaque bubble of depression I could not see through. I fought my way free. Not everyone can.

I know some people feel life has nothing left to give them. That is a place that I recognize. But the important question is not *What is life giving me? You must ask yourself what you have to give to life.*

Giving back does not require money, or even large amounts of time. The tiniest acts of generosity can have enormous effects. Buying a random person a cup of coffee, or helping someone at the grocery store reach for something when their arms are full, can offer a stranger hope for the future of humanity. Opportunities to hold doors for strollers or offer an arm to an elderly person crossing a street present themselves every day. Take hold of those moments and make them yours. Say *please, thank you,* and *you're welcome.*

Have faith in knowing you have a purpose, and watch for your moment. There is a reason for you to be here. An act of kindness only you can perform awaits you. It might be small. It might seem trivial or even unnoticeable to you but greatly affect someone else. Regardless of the number of people you impact, your legacy is valuable.

More people cared for me as an adult than I ever expected, or ever wanted. My mother ranks high on the list. When I was younger, I resented how she took over my care and my life, constantly trying to tell me what to do. Now that I have my own child, I can only begin to imagine what she went through.

In some ways, I think my epilepsy was harder for her than it was for me. I did not have to watch myself bleed from the mouth, turn blue, or scratch myself. I have never seen my eyes roll back in my head while I stop breathing, my body stiff and shaking as unnecessary amounts of electricity course through me. But my mom watched her child come close to dying over and over, powerless.

153

The hardest thing for me, and everyone who knows me, is my memory loss. The best advice I can give to caregivers as a person with no memory is *find patience*, and accept that your brain is different from theirs. If you have to deal with someone who suffers from memory loss, keep your perspective. Of course you must intervene if the person you care for cannot remember what a toothbrush is used for. But if they don't remember a movie you saw last month, or a trip you took as kids, let it go. Not remembering your beautiful wedding day does not make it less special. Focus on what is special about today.

For those struggling with disease, I encourage you to find your power. How do you face a new day when you open your eyes and know you will struggle every minute? Other than when we are in the moment, most people with seizure disorders look just like anybody else. Inside, our memory loss and exhaustion control our every waking moment. Keep in mind everyone else is a different color on the inside, too. Even people who are well carry baggage. Ours might be heavier, but that makes us stronger.

Combine little pieces of joy into the whole of yourself. When the ugly rears its head, as it is meant to do, remember you cannot stand in a valley if there is no mountain next to you. Climb the mountain, one tiny step at a time. When you reach the top, the struggle you left below will look small in the distance.

Encore—A New Day

Chapter 32—Texas

My father turned eighty in December 2017. As a gift, Brian and I decided to help him check something off his bucket list. The next summer, we took him, and Jake, to Garner State Park in Texas.

I came so close to revisiting my childhood twenty-seven years earlier, with my father, mother and boyfriend Craig. Now I would go not only with my father and husband, but with my son. I could see the river again through my child's eyes.

Jake loved it. Three other boys his exact age camped near us. He ran around and swam in the crystal water and stayed up late playing cards with a freedom city kids never experience. He and Brian swung from the ropes and jumped in the water. The river suffered from years of severe drought, flowing at a level too low for inner tubing. The shallow parts were too warm, and the spring box where we chilled watermelons was dry. But the long cement stairs and perfect jumping rock still matched the photos in my mind.

And, my dad's bucket overflowed.

After three days, we headed back to San Antonio. I made sure we all shared a decent hotel after three nights in a motor home that rocked like a ship and quickly roasted us in the Texas summer heat if we decided to turn off the a/c that roared like a wind turbine. I had to abandon my sleep schedule, and chose to ignore my non-dairy diet. The result was predictable.

When I opened my eyes, I could see Jake pacing the floor, his body contorted by emotion. I knew the sight. When our dog nearly died, Jake paced the same way, back and forth across the floor, terrified, not knowing what to do. Brian stood over me, talking gently to Jake. I heard my dad's voice, also calm and reassuring. They were all so awake—what time was it? I knew I couldn't speak, and attempted words might sound strange, so I didn't try. I gasped for air, unable to move. The sound disturbed even me, rasping, gurgling with saliva and probably foamy blood. My heart broke for Jake. He had never seen me have a seizure.

I surrendered to my disease, and sank back into sleep. Brian and my dad would have to handle this one.

We let Jake sleep while Brian got in the shower. My dad and I went down to breakfast.

We rode down in the elevator and got our hotel waffles without anything but pleasant chit-chat. Today marked the end of our journey, and we had travel plans to discuss. He was flying to Tucson that morning, and Jake and I were heading back to San Diego in the evening. Brian would drive the car home and arrive in a day or two. We talked about the great time we'd had, and the surprisingly good free hotel breakfast we were enjoying.

My dad and I never talked much about my seizures. He always chose instead to treat me like a perfectly normal person. I knew his reluctance to remember much about them stemmed from skillful denial, but I preferred our cheerful banter to serious musings about my disease.

"How often does that happen?" I could see it was difficult for him to ask. I steeled myself. I needed to have this conversation.

"It's been a very long time."

"Has it really?"

"Yeah. Really. I wish Jake hadn't seen it."

"Brian was amazing. He was so great with Jake. And with you." I could tell my father knew I was in good hands. That made us both feel grateful. "He couldn't have been better with Jake. Really."

"He's amazing."

"So amazing. The best dad ever."

My eyes began to feel heavy with tears. It's an emotional thing to hear your father say your husband is an even better dad than he. I shifted to the hard question I had to ask.

"Can you not tell Mom?"

My dad flinched. I was asking a lot. He paused before he answered. "Yeah. I will not tell her, if you don't."

"I won't." We both knew no good could come of my mother knowing. She would worry and fret and call me too often to ask if I was sure I wasn't having more seizures. She would be heartbroken to know Jake had seen the horror of what she witnessed so many times, feeling the devastating helplessness of watching me and not being able to help me.

"Are you okay?"

"I bit my tongue."

He nodded. "I know."

Of course he'd seen the bloody saliva foaming out of my mouth as I tried to pull myself back into a consciousness where my brain and body could communicate with each other. I really wanted to cry but I knew Jake and Brian would be down soon, and I couldn't have my son see me with tears running down my face. I needed to seem normal, and that did not mean crying, which he'd only seen me do twice.

I turned to my book, my sanctuary of clinical thinking, where I could describe myself as though I were a stranger. I pretended to interview my dad. "What was it like when I was having so many seizures? What do you remember?"

"You were always so out of it. And the drugs were worse than the seizures."

"Really?"

He nodded. "Some of them, you just sat with your mouth hanging open. You couldn't talk clearly, or remember words. You'd just stop, forget. It was bad." He looked out the window, shaking his head. "You went from performing improv comedy to staring at the floor, barely able to string two sentences together. It was awful."

We all went back to light conversation when Brian and Jake came down for their breakfasts. Jake ate quietly, not making much eye contact with me. He seemed unsure about how he should act, but quickly took cues from the rest of us, and tried to pretend nothing had happened. My father and Brian planned to leave before us, so I knew Jake and I would have one-on-one time to talk over lunch.

By the time Jake and I sat down together at a table at Rainforest Café we'd visited the Alamo and a few tourist traps. We'd laughed at squirrels and posed for photos. Everything was "fine." I probably could have avoided the topic forever and we would have gone on with our lives as if nothing had happened. That would have been so unfair to him.

"I heard you saw me have a seizure last night."

He answered without hesitating. "It was horrible. I wish I'd never seen that." He looked me in the eye and felt no need to sugar-coat his feelings. He came right out and said exactly what I was thinking.

"I wish you'd never seen it, too." It was so simple and honest; I didn't even feel like crying. "You know it's just my brain making too much electricity."

He nodded. I made sure he knew exactly what a seizure was, and why they happened, when he was five. But science didn't matter that day. "It was terrifying. You were making weird noises and you couldn't stop. It was like you couldn't breathe."

"I'm fine now, though. You can see that, right? I bit my tongue, so I might sound like I'm slurring my words a little, but I'm just me. I've had a lot of seizures in my life, and I'm okay. It's just part of who I am. I wish it wasn't, but we're really lucky that doesn't happen all the time like it used to, right?"

"Yeah. I don't ever want to see that again."

"I don't ever want you to."

I don't know if I will ever feel more close to my son than I did at that moment. He could tell me exactly what he thought and felt, and I could tell him how I felt, without needing to soften our words. It was beautiful.

Jake will always propel me forward. It is for him I truly understand the most important thing in my life—gratitude. However, to be here, always in the now, is a gift you can only give yourself. I don't need a past, with him in my present.

###

EPILOGUE

Over twelve million patients are misdiagnosed every year in the United States. That means one out of twenty of us will be given bad information by our doctors. Half of us, six million people, will potentially suffer great harm from being misdiagnosed. Medical misdiagnosis is now considered by some to be the third leading cause of death in our country. You are more likely to die from poor health care than from a car accident.

According to some sources, as much as seventy percent of these patients are women. Why?

The simplest way to examine the disparities between men and women when studying misdiagnosis is to consider information about our shared number-one killer—heart disease.

More women than men die from heart disease every year. However, the disease is not more prevalent in women. Why are women more likely to die? Because doctors treat them differently.

A woman who goes to a hospital while suffering a heart attack is seven times more likely to be misdiagnosed with stress or anxiety and sent home. A woman is also less likely to actually see a cardiologist at the hospital, and is more likely to present with what may be considered "atypical" symptoms.

Many of us have heard of the symptoms to look for when someone is having a heart attack. Tightening in the chest, pain radiating down one or both arms, sweating, and shortness of breath are classic symptoms. These "typical" symptoms are based on the classic patient: A 154-pound white male.

Doctors are trained to look for similar symptoms in men and women. But, physiologically, we are not the same. Our symptoms differ enormously.

Women can present much differently when suffering heart failure. They may have upper back pain, nausea and vomiting, or dizziness and fainting. Their preliminary test results are often considered atypical, as well. This should not surprise anyone, knowing the tests are not designed to accurately measure necessary data in women. The results for the treadmill test, for example, are set to reflect the normal expectations for a middle-aged man. The same results a man is expected to achieve cannot accurately diagnose a woman.

Even though medical professionals are aware of this glaring problem, not enough is being done to balance the disparity. Only twenty to twenty-five percent of patients in clinical trials for heart-disease research are women, despite the fact they are most at-risk for death from heart failure. Doctors are not learning to recognize gender differences, and women are suffering as a result.

Doctors are not the only ones who contribute to a higher death rate in women having heart attacks. Some blame belongs to all of us who are trained to provide CPR when we see a person in distress. Forty-five percent of men receive CPR from bystanders, but only thirty-nine percent of women are offered the same care. Perhaps we are all more hesitant to touch a woman's chest? A person who receives CPR in the early stages of a heart attack is two-to-three times more likely to survive. We cannot hesitate based on gender if we are thrust into that situation.

Several theories circle around the cause of the shocking number of patients not receiving proper medical care. The answer is most likely a perfect storm of several things combined.

Our insurance system bears a sizable portion of the cause. The one-size-fits-all model enforced by profit-driven medicine does not allow doctors to make thoughtful, intelligent diagnoses. Some doctors may even recommend more expensive tests, or may not recommend expensive tests, based on what the return might be from an insurer, rather than based on the needs of their patient.

Drug companies play an enormous role, as well. Doctors receiving money and incentives from pharmaceutical companies look for ways to prescribe certain drugs. They may choose a medication based on their own personal connection to a drug company, rather than based on the best choice for their patient.

These factors do not discriminate. Men and women all fall victim to "the system."

The real reason more women suffer from misdiagnosis is simply outdated gender biases. Just like we all have a certain vision when we hear the words "run like a girl," the words overemotional, hormonal, and in particular hysterical, all belong to women. Not surprisingly, women are diagnosed with mental illness forty percent more often than men.

Perhaps the problem is not just bias toward mental illness for women, but an under-served number of men treated for emotional and mental distress. Men account for seventy-nine percent of suicides in the United States. Ninety percent of suicide victims suffer from mental illness.

Just as typical symptoms of heart disease are based on the male physiology, mental illness determiners are based on female patients. For example, we all associate depression with sadness. However, in a man, depression often presents itself as anger. The constructs for recognizing and treating mental illness need to be updated to include typical male symptoms. If mental illness could be properly diagnosed in the male population, the gender-based disparity would shrink. With that, the stigma placed on women being too sensitive and overly-controlled by their emotions and hormones may change, as well.

Not only does the practice of over-using the diagnosis of anxiety or emotional distress put women at risk, it also diminishes the true conditions. Mental illness is a serious factor

163

overlooked by our healthcare system. Some estimate fifty-six percent of adults with mental health needs do not receive treatment.

Anxiety, separation and otherwise, is a condition that deserves to be taken seriously as it stands. It is not a dumping ground for every diagnosis that is not medically obvious. By lumping everything into this category, we are failing to properly define and treat mental illness. And, reflexively, other health conditions, particularly in women, are being under-diagnosed, or entirely ignored.

The implicit bias originating in antiquity with the first diagnosis of hysteria continues to plague women today. We face the danger of being gender-shamed every time we seek medical attention. The effects can be dangerous, devastating, and deadly.

I was a victim, and I could have died.

Finally, a few words about healthcare.

My parents had the means to pay for my insurance through my father's company, and to visit out-of-network doctors. It was very expensive. If they had not helped me financially, I could have died in my twenties with a diagnosis of anxiety disorder. I would not have had the money to pay my medical bills. I would have left this life under a heavy blanket of debt.

When you see people fighting our government over healthcare, they are fighting for their lives. They are fighting for their child's right to a second opinion, or a better test. They are fighting for the medications they need.

My former insurance company decided to drop my medication from their list. They sent me monthly letters suggesting I try Tegretol. After all I had been through to finally find a drug that worked for me, the insurance company decided they had a great drug for me to try based solely on the price of the pills. The cost of my medication went up to over $700. That, on top of the extra expense I paid for my insurance.

For a long time, I paid twice what my husband and son paid combined for lower-quality health insurance without drug coverage, even though I am a healthy, active person and had been seizure free for many years. I had a hard time finding a company to insure me at all.

Now thanks to the ACA, I pay a reasonable amount. I can keep my neurologist in Arizona. I am not a freeloader, taking advantage of anyone. I pay plenty for my insurance. I am simply able to go to the doctor for a physical, and to my neurologist for check-ups. I can go to a hospital and receive care if the need arises. That is not too much to ask.

The Varieties
of Epileptic Seizures

We are all electrical beings, and our brains are our bodies' batteries. When you scratch your head, rub your eyes, or run a marathon, your body is reacting to electrical impulses created by neurons in your brain.

Epileptics' brains are wired differently. Sometimes brains emit too much electricity, causing the body they are powering to seize. This might last for seconds or for hours, depending on the type of seizure.

One in ten people will have an epileptic seizure in their lifetime. Seizures can be caused by many other health conditions, including diabetes, low blood sugar, or brain infections. Epilepsy originates in the brain.

Seizures are not all the same. Based on where the electricity is discharged in the brain, and the length and strength of the electrical charge, seizures can look and feel very different.

During **focal awareness seizures** (FAS,) also called simple partial seizures, people are awake and aware of what is happening. I've known these as my *aura*, an indescribable sensation. FAS usually accompany or predict other types of seizures. They can present themselves as a strong sense of déjà vu, or a sixth sense.

Because I'm sleeping when I have seizures, for about ten years my aura came to me as a very frustrating dream: I'm in a hospital bed, and doctors are talking about me, rather than to me. They discuss my original diagnosis, talking about my mental illness. I sink into my seizure and begin to scream, or so I think. They do not notice me having a seizure. If I can actually find a way to wake myself during a FAS seizure, I can sometimes avoid a tonic-clonic seizure. But I feel like I'm tied down and have no power against the electrical force building momentum in my brain. My FAS probably lasts seconds, although it feels like minutes.

Absence seizures may look like "zoning out." They are most common in kids. A person's eyelids may blink or flutter, or they may stare blankly ahead. Although they appear to be awake, they are unaware of their actions and unable to interact with their surroundings. If they are on the move when the seizure begins, they can keep walking, but will not remember how they got from one point to another. These seizures pass quickly and do not involve unconsciousness.

Atonic and tonic seizures happen very quickly. In an atonic seizure, a person becomes limp and falls forward. In a tonic seizure, their body becomes stiff and falls backward. These seizures commence suddenly and end within seconds, and do not involve the jerking movements most of us visualize when we think of epileptic seizures. They can be mistaken for fainting.

Focal-impaired-awareness seizures vary depending on where they happen in the brain. A person may mutter nonsense, smack their lips, play with their clothing or wander aimlessly for a couple of minutes, or they may scream or make strange movements for fifteen to thirty seconds. They are semi-conscious and can react to their environment, but without full control of their actions. For example, if you try to subdue them, or you yell at them, they might respond by becoming violent and pushing you down. Afterward, they will not remember what happened during their seizure.

Myoclonic seizures are muscle jerks. The seizures I originally experienced, watching my limbs move without being able to control them, were likely Myoclonic (muscle jerk) seizures. Most people who have these also have other types of seizures.

Which brings us to **tonic-clonic seizures**. A person loses consciousness, their muscles jerk, they may bite their tongue or mouth, and they make strange noises and drool or foam at the mouth because they cannot breathe or swallow their saliva. Their bodies experience painful electroshock therapy delivered by their own brains. They become pale or turn blue, and they may lose control of their bladder. This lasts for a few minutes that feel like hours for everyone.

After the convulsions stop, the **postictal stage** of the seizure begins. No, it is not over when the jerking stops. This part of the seizure can last for seconds, or for hours. The postictal, or ending, part of a seizure is very personalized. My most common postictal symptoms are confusion, depression and sadness, frustration, exhaustion, and thirst.

Regardless of their individualized reactions, all people who suffer tonic-clonic seizures have a few things in common. During seizures, we are helpless, vulnerable, and spent. Our breathing eventually returns to normal, and our color returns. But memory does not. Pride and the concept of confidence momentarily disappear. We will not jump up and start right where we left off, as people with other kinds of seizures can.

You might have expected to see Petit Mal (French for "little bad") and Grand Mal (French for "big bad") on the list here. Those terms are no longer used. Petit Mal is now called "tonic," and Grand Mal is called "tonic-clonic." Also, "fits" are what children have when they don't get their way. Epileptics have seizures.

AFTERWORD

by Dr. Erin N. Castelloe, M.D.

If the doctors I sought care from had helped me instead of dismissing me, I may never have known the loneliness and fear that come from being a stranger in my own story.

~ Kate Recore

I met Kate Recore in 2010, the year her son and my twin daughters started kindergarten. While volunteering together at school book fairs or with the school foundation, we embarked upon an enduring friendship. Kate is not just my friend, a devoted mother, and a loving wife. She is a skilled teacher, writer, public speaker, debate coach, and—perhaps most importantly—a fierce defender of justice. I equally adore and respect her. I am humbled by her tenacity in not only surviving but painstakingly recreating years fragmented by uncontrolled seizures and staggering drug side effects. Her courage in crafting an unflinching portrait of herself when she was most vulnerable endows her with irrevocable humanity and authority, both of which she uses to empower others.

In the years since Kate first shared her story with me, I have grieved. In no predictable or logical order, I writhed my way through shock, outrage, despondence, and guilt to a disquieted, reluctant acceptance. Ultimately, I can accept Kate's story because she can, because it is part of her, and because she has transformed it into a powerful call to action. Yet, I do not accept that we—for I must include myself in the medical establishment—did our best for Kate. We must own and learn from our mistakes, be they personal or collective, or we will repeat them and doom future generations of patients to suffer from them.

I have always yearned to connect with those who are suffering and relieve—if not vanquish—that suffering; to reach out, clasp the hands of those drowning in malady-driven fear and loneliness, help them, and stand with them in the face of whatever might come. When I took my first job as a family physician in a reputable multi-specialty group practice, I thought I was finally on my way to achieving a lifelong dream. Unfortunately, I learned quickly that the compassionate, patient-driven care I wanted—and had been trained to provide—took more time than my group practice would allow, and a non-compete clause in my contract prevented my immediate retreat to solo practice.

(Castelloe E. "Finding Myself in Medicine."
Qualitative Research in Medicine & Healthcare,
(2017); 1:1-5, doi:10.4081/qrmh.2017.6301; and
Castelloe E. "Tincture of Time." *Qualitative
Research in Medicine & Healthcare* (2017);
1: 103-108, doi:10.4081/qrmh.2017.6925).

In medical practice, as elsewhere, time is money. Money is generated by seeing patients. In general, seeing fewer patients decreases earnings, and seeing more patients increases earnings. As a direct result, double-booking (booking two patients in a single appointment slot) is standard in large medical practices. When I worked in such a practice, I was frequently expected to care for a patient in seven or eight minutes or fall behind. (I fell behind.) At quarterly department meetings, physicians seeing eighteen to twenty patients per day (like me) were labeled *low producers* and advised to increase their *numbers*. That's it. To the system, I was not a physician but a *producer*, responsible for generating the revenue required for everything from keeping the lights on to paying the ancillary staff and administrators; and patients were not individuals in need of compassionate care but *numbers*, the means by which I was to generate revenue for the system. How did physicians become producers?

Perhaps the evolution of physicians into producers began with the migration of solo practitioners into group practices so that physicians could share costs, on-call responsibilities, ancillary staff, and facilities. Solo practitioners can buy a medical practice from an established physician and immediately assume care for the patients the practice serves; or they can start from scratch and work to attract patients to their practice. They must understand their costs, revenues, and the critical fact that their professional and financial success is dependent upon the care they provide and how satisfied their patients are with that care. If patients' needs are not met or their values are not respected, they will leave the solo physician's care (and the practice).

In contrast, solo physicians who join or coalesce into group practices are often immediately busy with large numbers of patients, progressively distanced from the costs and revenues of medical practice, and insulated against the financial repercussions of patient dissatisfaction, as dissatisfied patients may choose to see another physician within the same group practice rather than leave the practice. To ensure that physicians can focus on the medical care of patients, group practices typically hire business personnel to manage the group's financial responsibilities, insurance contracts, and marketing (including patient recruitment and satisfaction). This separation of responsibilities may seem like a good plan, even an excellent plan. However, as the number of non-clinical employees increases, so do the overhead costs of the group practice. As the overhead costs increase, so do the importance of maximizing reimbursements from insurance companies and the vulnerability of physician groups to declines in those reimbursements. Little by little, the insurance companies gain negotiating power. That power can grow and grow until the tail is wagging the dog.

171

In the United States, by and large, insurance companies, not patients, pay for medical care. Those who pay have great power in negotiating the terms under which they will pay. So, the insurance companies, not patients, choose the medical care for which they will pay. (In fact, even if you are un-insured or under-insured, the dictates of insurance companies impact you, as the type and quality of care that is widely available is driven by insurance-company contracts with large healthcare systems.) If you are *lucky* enough to have insurance, your insurance will negotiate contracts; those contracts will dictate which clinics you can visit, the healthcare providers you can see, the tests and procedures your provider can order, the medications your provider can prescribe, and the specialist referrals your provider can make. (Certainly, well-resourced patients are welcome to seek medical care independent of their insurance coverage, but most patients do not have the resources to do so.)

Healthcare systems receive reimbursement for the care they provide by translating that care into terms that insurance companies understand: International Classification of Diseases, Tenth Revision, Clinical Modification (ICD-10-CM) diagnostic codes and relative value units (RVUs). The more complicated and/or time-consuming a medical interaction or procedure, the higher the RVUs. For example, an office visit for a bladder infection in a young and otherwise healthy person will generate fewer RVUs than an office visit for chest pain and shortness of breath in an elderly person with numerous chronic medical conditions.

As more RVUs generate more income, healthcare systems squeeze their doctors to generate more RVUs in less time. This means doctors are scrambling to see as many patients as they can, as fast as they can. Then, they must spend countless hours (hours they could be devoting to patient- or self-care) documenting their work to the satisfaction of the insurance companies. If they don't document appropriately, the healthcare system won't get paid. If the healthcare system doesn't get paid, doctors don't get paid. It is a vicious cycle that starts and ends with insurance company profits, a vicious cycle that chews up physicians and patients alike.

Without patients, medical practice would cease to exist. Yet, the needs and values of patients—as defined by patients themselves—are not the central focus of medical practice. Rather, it is the *prescribed needs* of patients, as defined by powerful entities within the medical establishment (*e.g.*, insurance companies, physician organizations, practice guidelines, government agencies) that determine how medicine is practiced: the time a physician *should* spend with a patient, the tests a physician *should* order for a patient, the medications a physician *should* prescribe to a patient. Often, when a physician adds up all the *should*s to calculate what is *medically necessary* (i.e., the prescribed needs of the patient), the patients' intimate knowledge of their needs is a minor, perhaps negligible, consideration in the diagnostic and therapeutic plan.

Furthermore, physicians often fail to recognize or respect, let alone comply with, patient values. This may be the result of time pressures or physician characteristics, such as narcissism, over-confidence, and/or incomplete knowledge (a dangerous combination of which impacted Kate). Yet, when a physician fails to collaborate with the patient in developing a diagnostic and therapeutic plan that is consistent with the patient's values and with which it is possible for a patient to comply, that provider can formally blame the patient. A patient who fails to comply with the recommendations of a healthcare provider may be labeled *non-compliant*. There is even an ICD-10-CM diagnostic code (Z91.19) which will allow providers to bill/receive reimbursement for patient non-compliance. Though a patient may have a completely logical and defensible reason (e.g., intolerable drug side effects) for non-adherence to a recommended treatment plan, they may still be labeled non-compliant. This pejorative term, and the attitude that supports it, must be uprooted and eliminated from medical practice.

The pace, pressures, and attitudes of the profit-driven and pejorative healthcare system are also fanning the twin flames of physician burnout and suicide, and the expanding inferno threatens physicians and patients alike.

On January 13, 2018, in The Washington Post, in *What I've Learned from my Tally of 757 Doctor Suicides*, Dr. Pamela Wible (www.idealmedicalcare.org) wrote:

> *Assembly-line medicine kills doctors. Brilliant, compassionate people can't care for complex patients in 15-minutes slots. When punished or fired by administrators for "inefficiency" or "low productivity," doctors may become suicidal. Pressure from insurance companies and government mandates crush these talented people who just want to help patients. Many doctors cite inhumane working conditions in their suicide notes... Physician suicide is a public health crisis. One million Americans lose their doctors to suicide each year...*

I cannot prove that the physicians who saw Kate at the onset of her seizures (rapidly and incorrectly diagnosing her with an anxiety disorder, a label which haunted her medical records and further delayed an accurate diagnosis and appropriate treatment plan) fell prey to insurance company dictates or the pace, pressures, and attitudes of a profit-driven and pejorative healthcare system. Yet, my personal experience within the system feeds a nagging suspicion that Kate's misdiagnosis might have been avoided if just one of her physicians had *slowed down*, listened to, and believed Kate. Misdiagnosis and medical errors, while avoidable, are impossible to eliminate. The practice of medicine (despite scientific and technological advances) is an imperfect art, practiced by fallible human beings. However, by slowing down, physicians can and will reduce errors. In addition, by slowing down, they can give each patient a precious gift: time—time to be wholly present, listen, hear, perform a thorough exam, think deeply, collaborate effectively, and build trust.

I firmly and whole-heartedly believe that patients are a woefully untapped resource in the diagnostic process. Each

174

patient is the world's expert on themselves. Yet, instead of consulting the expert before them, a physician will often spend much of their patient-time staring at the computer-screen display of the electronic medical record (EMR), a resource which is often (in my experience and Kate's) incorrect or grossly incomplete. Physicians are forced to hurry. Listening to a patient may seem like an inefficient means of getting the information they want and need. Therefore, while a patient talks, a physician may half-listen while perusing or typing notes within the EMR. An invaluable opportunity to attend to and respect the patient (not to mention concentrate on the patient's detailed account of their medical concerns) is lost forever. The failure of physicians to focus on and be present to their patients contributes to misdiagnosis and mistrust. Both are deplorable and can, potentially, cause permanent or lasting harm.

Which is worse: misdiagnosis or mistrust? Consider two contrasting situations of misdiagnosis. First, imagine you have a physician you trust, who respects you and your time, who considers you and your values in their treatment recommendations. The physician you trust makes, despite their best efforts, a misdiagnosis, then recognizes the error and diligently works to arrive at an accurate diagnosis and a treatment plan that meets your needs. How would you feel about that physician? Now, compare that situation to one in which a misdiagnosis is made by a physician you do not trust, who you are hesitant to consult again, who does not respect you or your time, who rushes to an incorrect diagnosis and treatment plan, simply to get out of the room and on to the next patient. How would you feel about that physician? I'm guessing that you would choose to work with the physician you trust, despite the initial misdiagnosis. I know I would. I wish I could say that misdiagnoses and medical errors can be eradicated, but I simply do not believe that to be true. Nonetheless, I do believe that trust can be established and fortified—even in the face of misdiagnoses and medical errors—if we give our patients our most precious resource: time.

Yes, my outrage at Kate's story still burns from time to time, but it does not consume me. I hold her story—and my outrage—close to my heart because they fuel my determination to share my knowledge and my time with patients. Knowledge is power. I will share knowledge. I will share power. For Kate, of course. And, for any patient who honors me with their trust.

Made in the USA
Columbia, SC
20 March 2019